"I wish this book would be irrelevant.
I wish this book would be unnecessary.
But *The Unthinkable* is alarmingly relevant
and desperately necessary.

I thought the words in this book would have to
reflect the ugliness of its topic.
I thought the point of view of its author would
have to be shattered and crazy.

But the author of *The Unthinkable* has a true gift for writing.
In fact, dare it be said, the author has written an
extraordinary book about—the Unthinkable.

The author's perspective is, paradoxically,
both Shattered, as well as Whole.
It is therefore, in my view, genuinely Holy.

And the author is hardly crazy:
Her narration is personal, profound and gripping.
And her call to action is, in fact, a prescription for sanity.

I could not read this book.
I could not put it down."

—Arthur Kurzweil
American Author, Educator, and Publisher

"When two seventeen-year-old thugs slew an ambitious young woman, Susan Schaffer, in her own home, the crime wasn't just another story of gun violence in America. Susan's mother, Lois, made sure of that! *The Unthinkable* is a detailed account of Susan's life and a powerful narrative aimed at stopping "unthinkable" carnage. It is a profoundly brave and honest testimony that will move hearts and minds."

—**Rabbi Shaul Marshall Praver**
Newtown, Connecticut

"*The Unthinkable* is our contemporary *In Cold Blood* story, for that is how Susie died, in cold blood. Lois Schaffer captures the anguish in the aftermath of losing a child to gun violence. A mother, trying to make sense of a violent death of a kind, compassionate daughter, where there is none. It is a story that too many mothers in America share. Ms. Schaffer summons the courage to tell it."

—**Hon. Michelle Schimel**
New York Assemblywoman-Sixteenth District,
and Co-Chair of State Legislators Against Illegal Guns (SLAIG)

"This book is a powerful story about a tragic event that brought Lois's family to its knees. It's a story about gun violence at its worst. But, most importantly, it's a story about resilience in the face of adversity. I hope that it will inspire all of us to follow Lois's lead in a push to pursue real reform so that other families do not have to live the nightmare that hers has."

—**Kathleen M. Rice**
Nassau County District Attorney

"What Lois Schaffer has captured in *The Unthinkable* is the appalling resonance of gun violence, which shattered lives through three generations of her family. The brutal murder of her daughter has given a heart-rending passion and eloquence to Lois's voice in a book that calls out powerfully for an end to the gun culture that is fast becoming the most shameful manifestation of American exceptionalism."

—**Mitchell Rosenthal, MD**
Founder, Phoenix House

The
Unthinkable

Honor Non-Violence
and Diversity—

Lois A. Schaffer

The
Unthinkable

Life, Loss, and a Mother's
Mission to Ban Illegal Guns

Lois A. Schaffer

BROWN BOOKS PUBLISHING GROUP
DALLAS, TEXAS

The Unthinkable
Life, Loss, and a Mother's Mission to Ban Illegal Guns

Brown Books Publishing Group
16250 Knoll Trail Drive, Suite 205
Dallas, Texas 75248
www.BrownBooks.com
(972) 381-0009

A New Era in Publishing™

ISBN 978-1-61254-139-6
LCCN 2013950931

Printed in the United States
10 9 8 7 6 5 4 3 2 1

For more information or to contact the author, please go to
www.LoisSchaffer.com

For Susie

"You shall not murder."
—Exodus 20:13

"What greater grief can there be for mortals than to see their children dead?"

—Joan Didion

Author's Note

My purpose for writing this book is twofold: first, to relate the devastating effect of gun violence on the life of my daughter, our family, and friends who loved her and by so doing to raise readers' consciousness of the easy accessibility of guns and how they can end up in the wrong hands, either by accident or willful action, and second, to prevent tragedies such as our family experienced.

The primary focus of this book is to tell you about our daughter Susie who was brutally murdered, another victim of the scourge of the illegal possession of guns. The reader may ask why there isn't more information about the two young thugs who committed the crime in order to show the contrast between integrity and depravity. Though it was clear the perpetrators were out to break into homes and steal, no other information about their lives or family background was made available to help us analyze the reasons for their perversity. This information was unobtainable.

Even if such information had been offered, I still would have chosen to emphasize instead the life of a caring individual, my daughter, whom I've described from varying points of view in order to give the reader a clear understanding of the tragic consequences of gun violence. Insight into the perpetrators' personalities, family lives, and reasons for committing such a heinous crime became less important than a focus on guns, their easy accessibility, and their illegal possession which together cause instant, unwarranted destruction and heartbreaking human loss.

Acknowledgments

I offer my heartfelt thanks to the following people:

My mentors—the Honorable May W. Newburger, former supervisor of the Town of North Hempstead, and Evelyn Weinstein—in memoriam for their information and guidance.

Jean DeMesquita for sharing her political savvy.

Ruth Karter for her wisdom, advice, and listening with her keen mind and perception.

Debbie Heicklen who always found the time to help me with her illustrious computer skills.

Bobby Kurzweil for her encouragement and her shared passion to complete this work.

Muriel Weinstein, a first rate author whose advice and knowledge were invaluable.

Judy Cohen, my editor and a gifted writer, to whom I'm honored to refer to as a friend.

Janet Harris, Ph.D., my editor at Brown Books Publishing Group whose expertise and kindness were infinitely appreciated.

The Brown Books Publishing Group—it was a privilege to coordinate with Milli Brown, CEO; Beth Robinson, Acquisitions Director; Kathy Penny, Project Coordinator; Omar Mediano, Art Director; and Danny Whitworth, Designer.

Saul Turtletaub who suggested I write this book.

Alvin Glazier who always was and will be a friend and extended family.

Lois and Ben Lefton who are gifts.

Eric, my son; his wife, Nancy Reisman; and their three children, Jordan, Allie, and Ben who are sources of pride.

Rachel, Daniel, and Sarah—Susie's children who elicit joy and live in their mother's image.

David, my gentle husband, an extraordinary friend and partner. The blend of his sensitivity and legal brilliance is a blessing—unsurpassed.

Preface

Guns have many names—assault weapons, firearms, pistols, revolvers—but they all have the same potential effect: death. Martin Luther King Jr., John Lennon, John F. Kennedy Jr., Robert F. Kennedy—all American icons, were all victims of gun violence. Our society vividly recalls the 1993 mass shooting on the Long Island Railroad carried out by a madman. The gunman murdered Dennis McCarthy, Congresswoman Carolyn McCarthy's husband. Her son Kevin was permanently paralyzed, and James Gorycki died due to the same gunfire. These three men had become friends over the years as the result of traveling to work every morning on the same train. Congresswoman McCarthy's response to the tragedy was in the *Ottawa Sun*: "I know it's in the Constitution. But you know what? Enough! I think there should be a law—and I know this is extreme—that no one can have a gun in the US. If you have a gun, you go to jail. Only the police should have guns. It's ridiculous."

In 1999, the country was horrified by the mass shooting at Columbine High School in Littleton, Colorado, in which fifteen people died and twenty-three were wounded.

The mass murders in 2007 at Virginia Tech in Blacksburg, Virginia, resulted in thirty-three dead and seventeen wounded.

In 2009, there were thirteen dead and thirty-four wounded at the Fort Hood, Texas, mass shooting.

The nation was again rocked just after the New Year in 2011 when a deranged shooter opened fire on Arizona's Congresswoman

Gabrielle Giffords, seriously wounding her and killing five people, including federal judge John Roll and nine-year-old Christina Taylor Green.

Then in 2012, the nation saw a rash of gun-related deaths and mass murders taking place like a spreading cancerous growth.

February
A student at Ohio's Chardon High School, T. J. Lane, went on a shooting rampage. Armed with his grandfather's .22-caliber Ruger semiautomatic, he went to the high school, killing three students and injuring two others. On March 1, a *New York Times* article about the shooting written by Sabrina Tavernise and Jennifer Preston quoted neighbor and former sheriff Carl Henderson, who stated: "It was not unusual for guns to be kept in homes in this area." I was amazed when I read that Henderson also said, "It's too bad because no one would ever think something like this would happen." The "Stand Your Ground" law was brought to public attention as the result of George Zimmerman's shooting of seventeen-year-old Trayvon Martin in Florida. Twenty-four states have passed this law, giving individuals the right to carry semiautomatic weapons if they *reasonably believe* their lives may be in danger. Zimmerman had a legal gun permit, which is disturbing enough considering his history, but the "Stand Your Ground" law is a malignancy.

April
One L. Goh, a former student at Oikos University in Oakland, California, shot and killed seven people.

July
Devastation occurred at a movie theater in Aurora, Colorado. The gunman, James Eagan Holmes, dispensed tear-gas grenades

and then shot into the audience with multiple firearms, killing twelve and injuring fifty-eight.

August
Wade Michael Page, a US Army veteran, opened fire at a Sikh temple in Oak Creek, Wisconsin, killing six and injuring four.

October
Another shooting occurred at Salon Meritage hair salon in Seal Beach, California. The gunman, Scott Evans Dekraai, killed eight.

December
Kansas City Chiefs linebacker Jovan Belcher's murder-suicide in early December 2012 caused great anguish within the sports world and the nation. Belcher shot and killed his girlfriend, Kasandra M. Perkins, and then turned the gun on himself. Following this tragedy, noted sportswriter and newscaster Jason Whitlock wrote an article that correctly stated the obvious: "What I believe is, if he didn't possess/own a gun, he and Kasandra would both be alive today."

In mid-December, the nation was stunned when news spread of the deadly massacre at Sandy Hook Elementary School in Newtown, Connecticut. The gunman, Adam Lanza, was armed with three weapons when he went on a rampage that claimed the lives of seven adults and twenty children, who were only six to seven years of age. After seeing the arrival of first responders, Lanza committed suicide.

Emotions were visible throughout the nation. People stopped in their tracks on the street, some shaking their heads in disbelief, others conspicuously crying. This atrocity deeply affected everyone because so many of the massacred victims were innocent children.

The Huffington Post conducted a survey just four months after the Newtown massacre. The survey recorded more than 2,240 gun deaths during this time period due to homicides and accidental shootings across the United States.

Further heartbreak occurred on January 29, 2013. Hadiya Pendleton, a fifteen-year-old honor student at Chicago's King College Prep High School, was shot and killed while standing with her friends inside Harsh Park. The tragedy occurred only one week after she performed at the second inaugural events for President Barack Obama. The crime took place within a mile of President Obama's Chicago home.

The gunmen—Michael Ward, eighteen, and Kenneth Williams, twenty—confessed that Pendleton was not the intended victim. They mistook the group she was standing with for members of a rival gang. The two were arrested and indicted for multiple counts of first-degree murder, attempted murder, and aggravated discharge of a weapon in addition to numerous other charges.

In mid-August 2013, three trigger-happy teens, in Duncan, Oklahoma, shot and killed twenty-two-year-old Christopher Lane of Melbourne, Australia. Lane, an Australian collegiate baseball player, was shot in the back while he was jogging by Chancey Allen Luna, sixteen, James Francis Edwards Jr., fifteen, and Michael Dewayne Jones, seventeen. When questioned by the police about their crime, they said it was for "the fun of it."

There is a multitude of willful, intentional gun violence, but accidental deaths caused by guns also deserve mention. Indicative of this anguish was the unintentional shooting that occurred in Toms River, New Jersey, in April 2013. A six-year-old boy died after being shot by his four-year-old friend, who found a gun in his home.

David Hemenway, director of the Harvard Injury Control Research Center, conducted a study of accidental gun-related deaths from 2003 to 2007. Published in 2011, the study concluded that around six hundred and eighty Americans were killed accidentally by guns each year and that half of those victims were under twenty-five years of age. Further results indicated that children in the United States were eleven times more likely to die from an accidental gunshot wound than children in other countries.

"New Fashion Wrinkle: Stylishly Hiding the Gun" was the headline of a *New York Times* article on April 23, 2012, written by Matt Richtel. Mr. Richtel described in minute detail the growing popularity of garments manufactured to carry hidden weapons. Such a trend is beyond ludicrous.

At the Second Annual Sportsmen and Outdoor Awareness Day held in Albany's legislative office building on January 25, 2011, Assemblywoman Michelle Schimel, who has fought arduously for tighter gun-control legislation, delivered an appeal to the attendees just after the tragic shootings in Tucson. In an impassioned statement referring to the powerful gun lobby, she said:

> In light of the tragedy in Tucson, Arizona, it is my hope that discussions at the New York State Rifle and Pistol Association's Legislative Awareness Day will focus on advancing sensible legislation that will keep the public safe by preventing guns from getting into the hands of the mentally ill, criminals, and terrorists. The tragedy of Arizona is a case study of all that is wrong with American gun laws. Citizens must demand more of their federal and state legislators to protect them from rampant, unnecessary gun violence.

In an article published July 17, 2011, journalist Frank Bruni stated: "Massacre after massacre hasn't changed this nation's mind-boggling blitheness about guns." He was specifically referring to the newly elected, gun-toting, freshman Arizona state senator Lori Klein, who appeared just two days after the Arizona massacre for her swearing-in ceremony proudly showing off her Ruger. Senator Klein was questioned about her handgun, to which she replied, "Oh, it's so cute." Bruni responded in his article: "No, Senator Klein, it's a potentially deadly weapon. When are you and the rest of the country going to wake up to that?"

In 2008, State Senator Eric Schneiderman (elected in 2010 as New York state attorney general) partnered with Assemblywoman Schimel to sponsor the Microstamping Bill, which would require legislation to encode or microstamp bullets in order to trace their origin. Schneiderman and Schimel admit that microstamping will not prevent gun violence, but at least it will be a viable means to assist law enforcement in tracing gun ownership. The Microstamping Bill was passed by the state assembly but has still not been passed by the Senate.

A poignant example for the need to pass the Microstamping Bill was made after the horrific shooting of Maurice Gordon in June 2010. Gordon, an off-duty customs and protection officer, was shot twenty-five times. Twenty-five shell casings were recovered, but still his murderer remains free. With only anonymous shell casings as evidence, the Gordon family has been denied justice and closure.

Andrew Cuomo compellingly stated the necessity for microstamping on November 2, 2010, during his gubernatorial campaign. He said:

> We must keep our communities safe. Gun violence remains one of our most serious problems. We must enact common-sense safety laws, such as requiring the microstamping of guns. Microstamping, a pro-law enforcement, low-cost method of expanding the ability of police to identify guns used in illegal

activities, would require all new semiautomatic handguns to be equipped with microscopic identifying markings, which are transferred to each cartridge when the firearm is fired.

Tragically, we learn daily about ordinary citizens who are murdered. Gun violence is a cancer on our society that is growing unchecked. A single bullet can extinguish the life of an innocent person. In the mass shooting in Tucson, Arizona, little Christina Taylor Green succumbed to one bullet to her chest. Constant gun violence occurs in homes, on the streets, in places of worship, in shopping areas, and on high school and college campuses—all because of the easy accessibility of handguns. When guns end up in the wrong hands, we see suicides, accidental deaths, and homicides. Handguns are easily obtained. They are often stolen. There is the gun-show loophole where anyone can purchase a gun "no questions asked." We frequently read that someone on the police force was shot because a gun landed in the wrong hands.

After his election, New York's Governor Andrew Cuomo further emphasized his concern about gun violence. His speech at a breakfast in which he forcefully reiterated how gun violence has impacted the lives of every citizen in Harlem on November 18, 2011, was reported in the *Daily News*. "This recent rash of gun violence should concern us all, because it's frightening and it's only getting worse," he said. The governor made these concluding remarks: "It has been decades where we have been fighting Washington for sensible laws controlling guns, and we need those laws passed, and we need them passed now."

An individual's right to bear arms under the Constitution's Second Amendment has caused heated controversy regarding gun possession between the pro-gun and gun-safety advocates.

It is a war being waged against the growing number of deaths due to gun violence between reasonable people and groups such as the American Civil Liberties Union (ACLU) on the one side and the well-financed and unyielding power of the National Rifle Association (NRA) whose mantra is defense of the Second Amendment. Any concern the NRA may have to protect human life is outweighed by their almost fanatical desire to resist all regulation of firearms.

Leah Gunn Barrett, the executive director of the non-profit gun safety organization New Yorkers Against Gun Violence (NYAGV), said, "It's interesting to note that the NRA receives millions of dollars each year from gun manufacturers, so in essence it is an industry organization, not a public grassroots, public-advocacy/gun-safety organization. Their main reason for resisting common-sense gun laws is that regulations such as background checks would cut into gun sales. Making guns with safety features such as chamber-load indicators, triggers with enough pressure so a child cannot pull the trigger, Smart Guns that can only be fired by their owners, would mean additional cost. It's all about the bottom line."

Gun-safety advocates accept the right to bear arms for hunting and legitimate self-defense purposes. Shooting animals is one thing—shooting human beings is another.

Richard Aborn, activist and New York City attorney, has worked tirelessly to prevent gun violence. He was president of Handgun Control, Inc. (now called the Brady Campaign to Prevent Gun Violence) when the Brady Bill and the Assault Weapons Ban were passed. At present, he is president of the Citizen Crime Commission of New York City and a board member of New Yorkers Against Gun Violence. In 1993, Mr. Aborn stated, "The NRA claimed that they vigorously fought [the Brady Bill] at every turn and every step—because it was the nose of the camel [under the tent]. Today we would like to tell you what the rest of the camel looks like."

The gun lobby fiercely defends the Second Amendment right to bear arms. The National Rifle Association claims that guns should be owned by everyone as a matter of self-defense, asserting that therefore no deaths will occur. Such utter nonsense!

This salient point was expressed in Ellen Zelda Kessner's book *After the Violence*, which was written more than thirty years ago. The book, a wrenching account of the murder in Los Angeles of her twenty-eight-year-old daughter Sheryl, describes the brutality of her death and the extremist power of the National Rifle Association. Mrs. Kessner writes about the conversation she had with the district attorney after the sentencing of her daughter's murderer: "You still belong to Handgun Control?" he asked. Mrs. Kessner nodded her head to confirm that she did, surprised at the reaction of the district attorney, who repeated his NRA mantra: "If your son-in-law had a gun, your daughter would be alive today."

Mrs. Kessner continues to articulate this twisted thinking:

> Eleven years later, a double murder on my street confirmed the wrongness of this fantasy. Christmas Eve 1991, while my son's former classmate was fleeing from her dangerous boyfriend to cousins in the Bronx, her dad, a retired court officer, knowing the rifle-toting stalker would come looking for her first in his house, sat braced in his kitchen with his gun cocked. But the boyfriend broke down the door and shot him first. Then he shot his son, a court officer, too. Also armed.

This is America, supposedly a humane society, and yet we witness tragic deaths daily due to gun violence.

Sensible legislation is continually being explored by thoughtful people and organizations. One of the proposals is to initiate a waiting period before one can own a gun. In 1993, US Attorney General Janet Reno stated, "Waiting periods are only a step. Registration is only a step. The prohibition of private firearms is the goal." In that same year, Senator Charles Schumer of New York said, "We're going to hammer guns on the anvil of relentless legislative strategy! We're going to beat guns into submission!"

The Schumer and Reno quotes are humane but unrealistic in 2013 and just as uncompromising as the NRA. Gun safety individuals/organizations do not want to abolish legal gun ownership; rather the goal is to have reasonable discussions with gun lobbyists for sensible legislation. So it remains at a standstill.

Much has changed in the twenty-first century since the early 90s. Gun violence has escalated. The NRA has become more powerful than ever, adamantly unwilling to change their views regarding the Second Amendment. They consider background checks to be unconstitutional and, in some states, uphold the right to carry concealed weapons. Guns are sold at gun shows, no questions asked. The gun lobbyists believe if any of these measures is allowed, the "right to bear arms" will be "chipped" away. In 2009, *New York Times* journalist Bob Herbert stated, "We're confiscating shampoo from carry-on luggage at airports while at the same time handing out high-powered weaponry to criminals and psychotics at gun shows."

New Yorkers Against Gun Violence and the Brady Campaign are organizations noted for their intense commitment to sensible gun legislation. They understand that an individual has the right to hunt for sport and recreation, and they do not wish to prevent individuals from owning rifles with a legal permit for those purposes. Their focus is on preventing illegal handgun possession. Gun Free Kids is another organization that champions gun control, specifically focusing on the proliferation of guns on college campuses.

Kirsten Gillibrand, the junior senator from New York, was appointed by Governor David A. Patterson in 2009 to fill the US

Senate seat vacated by Hillary Rodham Clinton after she became US secretary of state that same year.

Senator Gillibrand was a resident of upstate New York, where guns were widely accepted, as was her embrace of the NRA's interpretation of the Second Amendment—which prompted them to grant her an A rating. Known for her campaigning expertise, Senator Gillibrand was twice elected to the United States House of Representatives from upstate New York's twentieth congressional district, and although a progressive democrat, she was an opponent of strict gun control. As a senator and a representative of the greater metropolitan New York area, she has made a sharp shift to the left, particularly on gun control. It is heartening to note that her focus is now on keeping illegal guns out of cities, tracking data on illegal gun traffickers, and closing the gun show loophole. She voted against allowing firearms to be checked in baggage on Amtrak trains, and she has now earned an F rating from the NRA.

Although she was originally a supporter of the NRA's interpretation of the Second Amendment, Senator Gillibrand's reversal on the issue of illegal gun possession will hopefully initiate stronger legislation.

In 2006, two mayors—New York's Michael Bloomberg and Boston's Thomas Menino—formed the coalition group Mayors Against Illegal Guns at Gracie Mansion in New York City. These two distinguished mayors serve as cochairs of the group, which now includes more than five hundred US mayors.

Yet, in 2013, in spite of valiant attempts to outlaw the possession of illegal handguns, brutal, senseless, gun-related murders are still committed with regularity.

Introduction

We live in a world of willful, unlawful violence. Gun violence has victimized many innocent people—not only those who are murdered but their families and friends as well. While mass deaths affect us all, we react more viscerally to the news of a young person's death, especially under violent circumstances. The impact is even more shattering when we know the victim personally. Such a death sears the very existence of the people who loved and valued the murdered individual.

My daughter's life was suddenly extinguished by gun violence on December 16, 2008. The devastating effect her death exerted and continues to exert on the lives of those who loved her emphasizes for us the compelling urgency to banish the scourge of gun violence largely perpetrated by the possession of illegal handguns.

Activists against the possession of illegal handguns say that the large number of deaths that occur can be translated in terms of thirty people per day, or the equivalent of a typical classroom of children.

Mayor Michael Bloomberg confirmed this statistic. The day after the Tucson shooting, he was invited to speak at the services of the Evangelical Crusade of Fishers of Men in Brooklyn on the first anniversary of the Haitian earthquake. He included the effects of the Arizona tragedy in his remarks, saying, "Thirty-four Americans are murdered—every single day. Tomorrow there will be another thirty-four. And so it will continue . . ."

Following is one personal story.

Chapter
1

"What the hell is going on here?"

Those were the last words Rachel heard her mother, Susie, say. They were talking on their cell phones. At first, Rachel heard rumbling, then cracking sounds. "Weird," she thought. Then the connection was lost. Rachel redialed her mother's cell phone. No ring. She tried again, but still nothing. Then she dialed her mother's home phone. It rang, and then all she heard was her mother's outgoing message on the answering machine.

Twenty-three-year-old Rachel was a practicing paralegal at a New York City law firm. Her mother lived in St. Louis and owned a newly opened exercise and fitness studio. Mother and daughter were chatting about their lives, respective work, and the weather. A major snowstorm had crossed the nation, resulting in frigid temperatures. Power outages and losses in electricity and heat were prevalent.

Rachel dialed her mother's cell phone again. No ring. She redialed the home phone. Again, she just heard the outgoing message. No one answered—not her seventeen-year-old brother, Daniel, not her sixteen-year-old sister, Sarah, and not her mother.

"Strange," Rachel said aloud to Stephanie, one of her coworkers.

"What's strange?" Stephanie asked.

"I was talking to my mom, and all of a sudden her cell phone conked out."

"Hmm, maybe it's due to the storm. I heard that many phone lines have been knocked out."

"Yeah, must be," she said. "But I heard things that didn't sound normal. I think I heard rumbling and then like a cracking sound. Then I *thought* I heard my mother say, 'What the hell's going on here?' as she was talking to me. Then her phone went dead."

"Why don't you try calling her again?"

"I did—several times."

"Try again."

Rachel redialed her mother's cell phone. Still no ring. She tried the home phone once more. Again, all she heard was the outgoing telephone message.

Chapter

2

These are the basic facts we know as given to us by the police. Kenneth Shepard and Lorenzo Wilson committed a burglary on December 16, 2008, and were interrupted by our daughter, Susie Schaffer. They were seventeen-year-old thugs who were just hanging out at Shepard's house because they were expelled from school for mischievous conduct. Shepard was also wearing an electronic bracelet that was supposed to keep track of his location.

The police characterized Wilson as "pure evil," a thug who had persuaded Shepard to come along even though Wilson had a gun in his possession. With nothing better to do, they decided to go on another rampage as they had in the past. Wilson boasted that he had found a gun, but Shepard was reluctant to accompany Wilson when he learned of it.

The police told us that Shepard and Wilson spent many hours wandering around the neighborhood, knocking on doors and ringing doorbells to see if anyone was home in order to break into a house, any house. They had no luck until they arrived at our daughter's house. We know that they tried to get in through the front door, but it was securely locked. The entrance through the back was accessible because the screen door was broken.

We also learned that upon entry Shepard heard the television set playing. When he was questioned by the police, he said he had wanted to leave out of fear that someone might be home, but Wilson convinced him to stay. Shepard walked into the kitchen and noticed Sarah's picture on the refrigerator. Again, he told Wilson he wanted to leave—he had recognized Sarah, who went to the same high school—and again, Wilson was adamant that they stay. Shepard told the police that Wilson insisted they stay because "they didn't come for nothin.'" He ordered Shepard to check upstairs while he looked downstairs to see what they could steal. They both rummaged through the house and took a camera, a laptop, and a cell phone that belonged to Daniel and Sarah, our grandchildren.

Wilson was surprised by Susie's unexpected arrival as he opened the refrigerator. Rachel was speaking to Susie on her cell phone as she interrupted the burglary and heard Susie shout "What the hell is going on here?"

Clutching the stolen items, Shepard bolted out the door. When Wilson spotted Susie, he shot her once. She collapsed onto the floor, and he shot her twice more in the back as she lay in a pool of blood. Then Wilson followed Shepard out the door, and both ran back to Shepard's house. Shepard later told the police that Wilson offered him the gun and said, "Now you take it and shoot somebody. I want you to know how it feels."

The congruity of this remark was startling. It was perversely repeated with different words but the same malice in August 2013 after the shooting in Duncan, Oklahoma, of Christopher Lane, the baseball athlete from Melbourne, Australia.

Both thugs were apprehended and subsequently jailed.

These are the bare facts. I can only imagine the horror Susie experienced during the last moments of her life. As agile as she was, she couldn't escape.

Chapter

3

Susie called me early in the morning on that fateful day to find out how we were doing after the snowstorm. She was getting ready to leave to teach at her Gyrotonic studio. We agreed that the snowstorm was over and that we could each attend to our daily routine.

"How're Sarah and Danny?" I asked.

"School's open and they're getting themselves ready to leave in-between watching TV. Come to think of it, I always have to remind them to turn the TV off. They remember to do that about 50 percent of the time."

"I know what you mean. They're young and couldn't care less about electricity costs."

"How's Rachel?" Susie asked.

"I guess she's fine. I assume she's off to work because I haven't heard anything to the contrary."

"Good. I'll call her later," Susie said.

Rachel called Susie while she was driving home from her fitness studio laden with bags of groceries from her weekly trip to the supermarket. Rachel later repeated to me what she remembered of the conversation with her mother.

"Mom was driving. First we talked about the snowstorm. We compared the differences we experienced for me in New York and Mom in St. Louis. She told me that although the snow had stopped, it was freezing, icy, and slippery. Many trees were uprooted. She was glad she didn't lose power but knew that many people were without light and heat. She made me promise to be careful about watching out for icy patches so that I shouldn't slip and fall."

"Sounds just like your mom."

"I know."

"Then what did she say?"

"We talked about Daniel, and she told me something that we thought was so cute about him."

"What was that?"

"He decided to get a haircut. She thought the only reason he would get one was that—at seventeen years old—he was in love. He was going to do it right after school."

"He's cute," I said.

"Then Mom told him she thought it was a good idea to get a haircut because he was so handsome and that way she could see his whole face."

"What did he say?"

"He said nothing, just blushed."

"And what about Sarah?"

"Mom called her 'a rip.' A sixteen-year-old who thinks she's thirty. I promised Mom I would talk to her and said that Sarah would be fine."

"You're right."

"But Mom wondered whether she would really be fine," Rachel said.

"Anything else?"

"Yes, I promised I would send her a new photo of me. She was noticing the pictures she had on the refrigerator. Sarah's and

Danny's were recent, but mine wasn't, and she wanted me to have a new photo taken. Then it happened."

"I know."

"It's hard to talk about it, but Mom was just pulling into the driveway, about to get out of the car. She told me she was going to keep talking while she walked into the house from the garage and then empty her groceries. I heard her gasp and at first couldn't believe what I was hearing. She actually did say, 'What the hell's going on here?'"

Chapter

4

Daniel returned home eager to show his mom his haircut. He trudged into the house through the garage, his heavy winter boots clomping on the floor as he entered. He heard the sound of the television set and remembered that he had forgotten to turn it off when he left for school that morning. Passing the laundry room on his way into the kitchen, he yelled, "Ma, I'm home."

As he entered the kitchen, he experienced the greatest shock of his life—a shock that rendered him totally speechless and immobile. He saw his mother lying motionless and face down on the kitchen floor, blood oozing from her body and trickling toward the kitchen cabinets.

Daniel dropped to his knees. "Ma!" he screamed. But she didn't move or speak and didn't seem to be breathing. Somehow, Daniel managed to pull out the cell phone he was carrying. He called 911, then Alvin (his mother's longtime partner), and finally, his father. While waiting for the EMT unit to arrive, Daniel lay on the floor next to his mother, stroking her, kissing her, speaking to her, and trying to rouse her.

The EMT unit and Alvin arrived at the same time. The EMTs suggested that Alvin and Daniel wait outside while they tended to

Susie. Alvin put his arms around Daniel and they held each other in desperation as they stumbled outside through the bone-chilling air and into Alvin's car. They sat together in stunned silence until Alvin managed to ask, "Do you know what happened?"

Daniel hesitated for a moment, and the only words he could utter were, "My mom's not breathing."

Suddenly, Daniel's cell phone rang.

"Yes, Sarah."

"Where's Mom? I'm at my friend Laura's house, and I've been trying to call her on her cell phone. It's dead."

"Sarah, I can't talk now."

"Why? Is something wrong? You sound weird."

"Just stay where you are. I'll come get you later." He closed the phone. Daniel and Alvin huddled together to keep each other warm and to bolster their emotional strength.

They waited and waited in the car, both of them freezing and trembling at the thought of the horrific news they feared was only minutes away. Alvin managed to compose himself enough to initiate a chain of phone calls to our family in New York. First he called my husband, David. In clipped speech he said, "I can't talk long. Something terrible has happened. I'm sitting in the car with Daniel." Losing his composure, he screamed into the phone, "Susie's been shot!"

David spat out the words, "Who? When? What?"

"Oh God, oh God! I don't know! I'll call you later when I have more information."

David immediately made a conference call to me and our son, Eric, trying to remain as calm as possible. "There was an intrusion in Susie's house. The EMT unit is working on her."

"What happened?" I asked as an ominous feeling crept into my chest.

"I don't know. All I know is that Alvin just called me with the information I just gave you."

"Dad, maybe she'll be all right. She *has* to be all right."

Eric's voice was barely audible, and both David and I knew he was crying though he was making a valiant effort to conceal it from us.

"From the sound of Alvin's voice, I'm very worried," David told us. David had always maintained a thoughtful, calm demeanor, but now his anxiety was clear. "Both of you, stick close to the phone. I'll call you after I hear from Alvin again."

David called ten minutes later, his speech almost unintelligible. "She's dead. Our daughter is dead."

A strange numbness pervaded my body, as in a suffocating nightmare. All I wanted to do was scream, but I couldn't.

"What—what are you saying to me?" I finally shrieked into the phone.

David's voice quavered as he delivered a message that no parents on earth should ever hear: "Susie was shot. Murdered. She's gone," he choked out through his tears.

In disbelief, not knowing where the self-control I summoned came from, I said to David, "I don't want you to drive home in such a state. How are you going to get home from the office?"

"One of my partners will drive me home," he managed to answer.

"You need to call the airline to get on the first flight we can to St. Louis tomorrow for the two of us, Eric, and Rachel."

"I've already done that. Also, Alvin told me that his sister, Lois, is opening her house as a meeting place for everyone."

News traveled quickly. Neighbors arrived in tears, offering help and support. These were people we had known for the thirty-plus years we had lived in our home, people who had watched Susie grow from a teenager to an adult.

David arrived home with his partner. There was nothing to say. We just hugged each other as hard as we could.

Soon Rachel appeared. "I can't cry," she said. "It's unreal."

Eric and his wife Nancy arrived soon after that. Eric said nothing. His red, swollen eyes said it all.

Chapter

5

Our family's life was irrevocably changed on December 16, 2008. On that day, my wonderful daughter, Susie Schaffer, had her life savagely extinguished by a young punk with a gun.

She was a vibrant human being with a personality that mixed strength and softness, a blend of focused grit and sensitivity, sometimes mischievous and often outspoken.

Susie first demonstrated her outspokenness when she was three years old. I was talking to an elderly lady who unfortunately was missing her top front teeth and whose hair was stringy and in disarray.

Susie studied her while we were talking. All of a sudden, her little voice piped up. "Are you a witch?" she asked innocently. I quickly clamped my hand to her mouth. Luckily, this woman was hard of hearing.

Her grit manifested itself when she was a young child as well. She could be tough as nails, but at the same time, she was sensitive to other people's feelings. This balance was demonstrated in an incident when she was eight years old and in grammar school.

One of the boys in her class kept making fun of her name. He called her "Schaffer beer," repeating it continually and annoying

Susie to no end. She warned this boy that if he didn't stop, she would let him have it. Finally, one day she had enough of his nonstop name calling.

The school day had ended. Holding her briefcase, Susie was walking home from school and this boy was behind her yelling "Schaffer beer" over and over again. Susie whipped around on her heels and without hesitation kicked him in his shins so hard that he doubled over. But that was not enough for Susie. She hoisted her briefcase and swung it at the boy as he was doubled over, saying, "I warned you." She ran home and burst into the house just after I received a phone call from the boy's mother.

We talked about it later. I remember Susie at that tender age revealing her sensitivity to me about her feelings and this bully. "He hurt my feelings all the time," she said. "I didn't want to hurt him, but I finally had to do something."

And Susie did. That kid never called her "Schaffer beer" again.

When people spoke with Susie, she looked into their eyes, and you could almost see her absorbing every word they said. Her interest in others was evident, and her sincere smile lit up her face whenever common ground was reached. It's a cliché, but to know her was to love her.

Susie was even lovable in spite of her housekeeping deficiency. She attended to the laundry and kept the house as clean as possible, but shoes, clothing, and papers were always lying about. Annoyed by the clutter, Rachel and Sarah voiced their concerns to me. I told them it was something they couldn't change, although they could help their mother by keeping their own rooms neat. I also pointed out that if she had the choice between spending more time on housekeeping and cooking a delicious meal for them, the latter would win. The disarray in the house didn't matter as much to Susie as time spent exercising, satisfying her children's palates, and sustaining their nutrition.

To me, the most important aspect of Susie's personality was her profound concern with accomplishing projects for the "greater good." These pursuits included activities such as volunteering in Barack Obama's 2008 presidential campaign. Phone calls rang back and forth from our home in Great Neck to hers in St. Louis on election night. She called us that night, crying, then laughing, then screaming into the phone, "He made it! He made it!"

She volunteered her time in the St. Louis public schools where she taught exercise classes and spoke about the need to maintain physical fitness. Even when she had a grueling schedule, she soldiered on because she loved her profession and she loved children.

In the spring of 2007, she completed another important project. She opened a new Gyrotonic exercise studio in St. Louis, finally realizing her dream of owning her own business. She was overwhelmed with happiness now that she was able to continue her passion for teaching, exercise, and nutrition.

Her passion went well beyond simply exercising. It included promoting healthy living for herself and others and supporting breast cancer research. She became aware of breast cancer in early childhood upon learning that her paternal grandmother had died of the disease. She learned that the disease could possibly be prevented by eating the right foods and exercising regularly, a theory she eagerly shared with her friends and students. Susie's enthusiasm was contagious. She convinced her students that the search for a cure for breast cancer was imperative, whether anyone in their families had the disease or not. She consistently donated a part of the fees she received to breast cancer research and considered it her way of giving back for the professional success and personal fulfillment she was experiencing. Many people gladly contributed, not only because they believed in the cause but also out of respect for Susie and her dedication to finding a cure. When Susie counted the many hundreds of dollars everyone donated, she felt both gratified and grateful.

Susie's project was emblematic of her determination to do the right thing. "Acting responsibly" was a phrase she heard repeatedly throughout her life. Her grandmother and I spent much of our adult lives in political activism and in helping others on both community and national levels. This expression, however, was driven home perversely during the spring of 2006.

It was a little warmer than usual for mid-May in St. Louis, and the warmth of the sunshine on Susie's face felt soothing after a long day of teaching. She headed to the supermarket to pick up food for the two children who still lived at home with her, fifteen-year-old Sarah and sixteen-year-old Daniel.

Susie parked her car in the supermarket's lot, found a shopping cart, and checked the list of items she and her long-time partner and soul mate Alvin had compiled during the week. Sarah and Daniel were growing teenagers with huge appetites who were conscious of their mother's focus on eating healthy foods.

The shopping cart was brimming with items, particularly foods she knew Sarah and Daniel would like for their school lunches and dinners. After everything was checked out, she looked forward to going home and preparing the evening's meal.

"Where's my car?" she mumbled. She walked up and down the parking lot aisles. No car. Again, she walked up and down, but still could not spot her car. She started perspiring as she pushed the heavy shopping cart yet a third time around the lot.

Maybe I just think I parked it in this aisle, but didn't. She wondered if her car had been stolen and whether she should call the police. But then she suddenly spotted it and immediately expressed several epithets that were worthy of a seasoned sailor. No wonder she didn't recognize her car. Someone had backed into it with such force that the rear end was completely concave and both taillights were smashed to smithereens. She tried to open the trunk to deposit her groceries, but that was impossible. After swearing again in sheer frustration, she looked around to see if anyone might have witnessed what happened, but no one was in sight. She rushed to the front of the car to see if anyone had left a note. Nothing.

"Who the hell would do this and just walk away?" She quickly emptied the shopping cart onto the back seat, front seat, and floor and started for home. On the way, she was able to take a few deep breaths and think with a cooler head about what had happened. First, she reminded herself that cursing was pointless, as she always told her children. On the other hand, she rationalized that in this instance she was entitled to a few salty words. Second, what had happened violated her principle of personal responsibility. She considered it indefensibly irresponsible of the person who smashed her car not to have at least left a note.

That night at dinner, she related the incident to Alvin, Sarah, and Daniel. "First, I got annoyed when I couldn't find my car," she said. "Then I began to worry that it might have been stolen. I was tired, hot, and pushing this heavy shopping cart."

"I can just imagine your frustration," said Alvin in his usual thoughtful manner.

"After I saw that the driver didn't leave a note," Susie said, "I had a few choice words for him—or her."

Alvin, Sarah, and Daniel smiled at each other, familiar with Susie's outrage at injustice.

"Yeah," she continued, "I remember my mother telling me that resorting to gutter language was wasted energy. Better to use that energy to do whatever was needed to rectify the situation. But considering the circumstances, my mouth got the best of me. Tomorrow I'll take the car into the service station."

"Bummer," Daniel said. "Whoever backed into your car must have been driving a truck or a large van because your car isn't a light one. That guy must have hit it pretty hard to dent it so badly."

Sarah laughed. "The dent makes it look like one of those steel drums you can play music on."

They all laughed at Sarah's response. As a teenager, she sometimes had an odd way of looking at things.

The car was repaired several days later. The service station attendants and mechanics had known Susie for many years and had always admired her for her kindness and energy. They also appreciated her sense of humor, teasing her about her muscles and knowing she would tease them right back.

"Yeah," she would say, winking and with her usual smile, "I got muscles, and you better behave yourself because if you don't, you'll feel my muscles in ways you don't want to."

They gave her a discount for the repairs and a free loaner car. The repairmen treated Susie with respect, not unlike the responses she received from other merchants she dealt with: the local cleaners, restaurant workers, the wine merchant, the cheese store employees, and the supermarket employees. She always treated others with the friendly respect that was second nature to her, and people always responded in kind. Over the years, she had built strong, warm relationships with everyone she came into contact with. People would see her and rush over to give her a hug. It was obvious why she elicited these feelings. Susie was genuinely interested in their lives and families and listened keenly to them when they confided in her.

Chapter

6

Susie was as beautiful as she was healthy. Her curly red hair, greenish eyes, and long, lean body attracted attention. When she passed people on the street, she saw them smile as she walked by. But it wasn't Susie's style to put herself on display. She was modest by nature. At forty-eight, her lithe body was like that of someone half her age. She had worked hard to maintain her strength and fitness because it was important for her to be healthy. As a fitness instructor, she wanted to be a role model for others.

People didn't believe her when she confessed that she once was "really fat" and fifteen years earlier, after her last child was born, she had gone on a demanding diet, exercise, and strength-building regimen. Many people asked about her amazing fitness, and she explained that she had always participated in different kinds of movement techniques. She was a swimmer and runner from childhood on, and also took countless aerobics and dance classes at the renowned Martha Graham School of Contemporary Dance.

The exercise was easy enough for her. But the eating—that was another story. "I could pack it away," she would tell people. "I liked to eat entirely too much." She knew she needed to work on curbing her voracious appetite.

During her teenage years, Susie once questioned me about her eating habits as a child, because she thought she looked chunky and was unhappy with her weight gain. "Ma," she asked, "was I a problem eater?"

"There were foods you didn't like, but I didn't want to force you because that might have completely turned you off to appreciating good food."

Without skipping a beat, Susie answered, "Why didn't you force me?" Damned if I did or damned if I didn't.

The diet, exercise, and strength-building regimen Susie embraced as an adult, in addition to the aerobics classes she taught, helped her to slim down. But it was not until she met Alvin, an accomplished personal trainer and walking encyclopedia of nutrition and body mechanics, that she completely committed herself to a lifestyle encompassing healthy eating and exercise.

Alvin had so many wonderful attributes. He was gorgeous inside and out, and with him Susie blossomed as she had never done before. He was over six feet tall, and Susie looked up to him, both figuratively and literally. His brown, curly hair was matched by deep-set brown eyes that focused intently on the person he was talking to.

Alvin became the love of Susie's life after she quickly discovered that besides being good-looking he was also a kind, considerate man who shared her intellectual, political, and spiritual values. He appreciated his identity as a Jew just as she did, which added a special dimension to their relationship. It was also a refreshing change from her former husband's complete lack of interest in acknowledging his birthright.

During a weekend visit to St. Louis, David and I witnessed an incident that was upsetting for Susie but emphasized her respect for her Jewish identity. At the time, Daniel was seven years old,

Sarah was five, and Rachel, who was studying for her Bat Mitzvah, was twelve. The three children had spent the previous day and night with their father and his wife, Dee. When the children were returned to Susie's home on Sunday afternoon, Daniel announced, "We went to church." Susie thought he was joking and laughed. But Daniel repeated, "We went to church."

Susie looked at Sarah, then at Rachel, and asked, "Is this true?"

"Yeah," replied Rachel, "but I wouldn't go."

Speechless for a moment, Susie finally asked, "So why did this happen?"

"Ma," answered Rachel, "this was the deal. Either I stayed home to take care of Daniel and Sarah or I went with them too. I can't handle the two of them alone, and why would I want to go to church?"

"So what did you do?"

"I stayed at their house. Sarah and Daniel went."

"I'm not thrilled about that."

"It was fine, Ma. I'm almost thirteen."

"I know that. But still, it was not the right thing for your father to do. And why did your father go to church? He's a Jew! He may not care, but he *is* Jewish—or is he converting to Catholicism? He's your father and supposed to be there for you!"

Susie raced to the phone while the three children, Alvin, David, and I watched her. You could almost see fumes coming out of her head.

"Susie," Alvin said, "calm, calm." He lowered his hand as emphasis.

"I know," she replied. "I'll try to remain calm, but I'm furious."

"It's negative energy," Alvin said. "I understand your frustration, but for your own good, try to keep your cool."

Susie looked at Alvin for a moment and then took a deep breath. She picked up the phone and angrily punched in the telephone numbers.

"Peter, whatever possessed you to take the children to church?" A pause while she listened. "You had to go? What do you mean, you had to go?" In rapid fire, Susie continued, "You always complained about going to services at temple! Now you willingly go to church? You were supposed to be taking care of *your* children!"

Susie grimaced in disgust while she listened, then managed to say, "Peter, now listen to me. I'm saying this loud and clear. If you ever do that again, you'll never have another opportunity to see them!" She slammed the phone down.

We all looked at one another, knowing Susie meant to keep calm but also realizing that in the heat of the moment it was emotionally impossible for her to do so. She held absolute commitment to her heritage and its significance for her children. The value Susie placed on her Jewish heritage was not based primarily on religious beliefs, but rather on cultural and, even more important, humanistic values. Alvin held strongly to the same beliefs. An added attraction, as Susie often remarked, was how much Alvin reminded her of her father, who is also smart, kind, and active.

Susie discovered that in addition to Alvin's athleticism, compassion, and intelligence, he was worldly, had traveled abroad, and had a fluent command of Spanish. She once asked Alvin how and why he gained this fluency. It was a beautiful romance language, he told her, but it was also a way to establish meaningful connections with the many Hispanics he knew who could not speak English. Alvin also had the capacity to make Susie laugh so hard that her stomach muscles had a real workout. He had a gift for telling stories in many different dialects, rendering her helpless with laughter. She continually remarked that if she closed her eyes, she thought an actual foreigner was spinning those tales.

Susie was also drawn to Alvin's sister, Lois, and brother-in-law, Ben, in addition to their children, Elizabeth, Lauren, and Scott. They were a warm and welcoming family, whom Susie found charming.

She had grown up in New York, and in St. Louis she often missed the large gatherings of family and friends that we hosted in our suburban home. Alvin, Lois, and Ben filled that family gap for Susie; they welcomed her and her children into their family.

Chapter

7

Three modes of thought and action governed Susie's personality. One was her respect for her Jewish heritage and determination to instill the same in her children. The other two were unconditional love and unswerving dedication to doing the right thing. This was how she lived.

Shortly after she and Peter moved to St. Louis, an incident occurred that clearly demonstrated the pride she derived from her Jewish identity. Peter had joined a medical practice and was the only Jew. This posed neither a problem for the doctors in the medical practice nor for Peter. An issue arose when a reception was scheduled for the doctors and their wives at a private club, which Susie learned restricted Jews from access. Susie voiced her objections about going to such a club, although it didn't bother Peter. The question in Susie's mind was whether to violate her principles as a Jew or be the dutiful wife and attend. Much discussion ensued among Susie, Peter, and us. She concluded that her appearance at the reception was the proper thing to do; she would support her husband, even though she was violating her principles. Ultimately, and ironically, she couldn't attend because at the last minute their sitter was unable to come.

Susie always spoke to her children about the unconditional love we showed her even when she misbehaved or made a choice we did not approve. Conversely, Susie's ex-husband Peter, the product of a contentious divorce, did not experience the unconditional love she had been raised with.

Peter had a perfunctory relationship with his mother but was totally estranged from his father. They hadn't spoken in many years. Before their wedding, Susie tried to convince Peter to call his father with news of their marriage, but he refused. She was thoughtful enough to make him sit down with us as we tried to persuade him. He listened, but he never did it because he was so full of anger toward his father. Susie wanted Peter to make this call not only because it was the right thing to do but also so he would not have regrets later in life. Holding onto his anger, he never was able to do it. Susie also wanted him to share with his father about his successes in medical school. Peter had become a highly skilled neuroradiologist. Again, he refused.

The same anger pervaded Susie and Peter's divorce. Although we were in-laws, Peter had regarded us as friends. He respected the fact that we were a couple who loved and liked one another. He especially respected David for his brilliance, kindness, and strength. All that changed drastically after the divorce, when we became the enemy.

For the first five years of Rachel's life, Peter doted on her. After that, there was nothing but put-downs or criticism. That treatment escalated as she matured, deeply affecting and confusing Rachel. Peter transferred the anger he felt for Susie onto Rachel and Sarah, treating them rudely at first and ignoring them as time went on. As a result, Rachel refused to share anything with her father in the same way Peter had refused to share with his own father. Their strained relationship was particularly evident during Rachel's Bat Mitzvah.

Susie called me just a week before the Bat Mitzvah to pour out her heart. Peter had refused to participate in the ceremony, and Susie felt strongly that if it was not pleasurable for him, it should at least be his parental obligation to take part in this milestone.

"Ma, I don't know what to do. I've spoken to him countless times, and he has no interest. There's less than a week left before the Bat Mitzvah."

I listened intently and asked, "What is it he needs to do besides just show up? I know he doesn't know how to read Hebrew, but he could say the prayers in English."

"Yes, he can read the English when he's called to the *bimah*. But in our temple, each parent is asked to speak to the Bar or Bat Mitzvah child as part of the service. He doesn't want to do that."

"That's a problem."

"Tell me about it."

I could sense the frustration in Susie's voice.

"This is his daughter. He shouldn't punish her based on how angry he is with me."

"I agree, but what can we do about it?"

"Ma, I'm going to talk to the rabbi. He's super understanding, and I know he can help."

"Great idea."

"I'll let you know what happens."

Susie called several hours later sounding more relaxed.

"This is the story. I spoke to the rabbi. He called Peter and reasoned with him. He emphasized the importance of participating, not for the religious significance, which he knows that Peter doesn't give—excuse my language—a four-letter word about, let alone his appreciation of his Jewish identity. The rabbi just persuaded him to do it for parental support."

"So what happened?"

"He's doing it—reluctantly, but he agreed to do it."

"Thank goodness for that," I said, relieved.

"Ma, you know it's the right thing. Rachel is his daughter and love should be unconditional."

There were other instances of dissension between them over the years. Rachel did not include Peter in the decision when she chose a college, which angered him. His resentment increased two years later when she transferred from the University of Colorado at Boulder to Hofstra in New York and didn't tell him until after the fact. After the third year, Rachel dropped out of Hofstra because she had misunderstood the information about her aggregate credits. David, Susie, and I believed that Rachel's heart was not in pursuing a college education. In essence, she may have been subconsciously getting back at her father for the lack of approval throughout her teenage years, which was a complete reversal compared to his loving treatment of her as a child.

I vividly recall one evening at dinner when Susie, Eric, David, and I tried to persuade her to return to school. Susie told Rachel that there were times when college had become difficult for her and she had wanted to drop out as well, but didn't. Rachel looked at her mother straight in the eye, pointed to David, and said, "Yes, but Ma, look at what you have and I don't." Apparently, the return to Hofstra or any college would have meant a fifth year, which Peter refused to subsidize. This state of affairs was very sad. It was gathering momentum, rolling along like a snowball and just as cold.

Later I realized that human nature is an enigma. People tend to focus on what they don't have rather than all that they do. Rachel had a mother, grandparents, and an uncle who always praised and encouraged her, but what remained uppermost in her brain was the disapproval she received from one person, her father.

Rachel negotiated an alternative plan that Peter finally agreed to. She applied to Hofstra's paralegal program and was immediately accepted. Concurrently, she was hired to work in a nearby law firm as a paralegal assistant while she attended school.

We were heartened to see Peter show signs of acting like a caring parent after Susie died. Rachel was living and working in New York as a paralegal at the time. Peter asked his three children to come live with him and his wife, Dee, a compassionate individual and a buffer between the girls and Peter. He volunteered to pay for Rachel's return to college in St. Louis and even subsidized an apartment rental for her, admitting that a twenty-four-year-old needed to live independently. He made every effort to be physically and emotionally present for his children. I could almost hear Susie's words "unconditional love" and "doing the right thing" come back.

We were also pleased to see Peter's willingness to help David when he learned that David was experiencing excruciating sciatic pain in his leg. Peter offered to view his MRI film that was taken in New York, and we had the film sent to him. He called David several days after examining the film and suggested that David see a specialist he knew in St. Louis who had achieved success with such cases by administering epidural injections. Conversations and e-mails went back and forth between the two of them. Ultimately, David opted to have surgery and Peter concurred. He called David a few days after the surgical procedure.

"How are you feeling?"

"Great and pain free."

"So we know it was the correct route to take."

"Yes," answered David, "and thanks for your interest."

One can only hope this kind of communication continues with us and the girls. Susie would have said, "It's doing the right thing."

Chapter
8

Alvin first met Susie while they were both teaching at the same fitness studio. Her given name was Susan, but our family lovingly called her Susie, and the nickname seemed fitting for someone with her spunk and sensitivity. During their fourteen-year relationship, Alvin also referred to her as Susie or Suze. When they met, he had been hearing about her for several years. He knew that she was recently divorced. As a personal trainer who moved in some of the same circles that she did, Alvin learned that people had the highest regard for Susie. Based on her passion for helping others, she was known as a role model in her appearance, her athleticism, and her position as a respected fitness instructor.

One day, Alvin saw her as he happened to pass by the studio where she was teaching and had to stop because he was captivated by how she conducted the class. A curly redhead with a long, lean, muscular body, she was just as people had described her. She was teaching an exercise class in the same fitness studio that some of Alvin's clients attended. As he watched the class, he could see why she was so much admired. She had impressive physical flexibility, demonstrating all the movements she described. There was also a warmth about her that was easy to see. Alvin noticed how she walked around the crowded classroom, smiling and gently helping those who needed it. He stood and watched until the class was over, and he was touched by the people in her class kissing or hugging her before leaving. When the room emptied, Alvin walked over to Susie as she picked up her handbag.

"Hi, my name's Alvin, and that was some great class. I'm a personal trainer, and after watching your class I think you're about the most flexible person I've ever seen."

"Thanks. I had a lot of dance training, so it figures that I'm flexible."

"Still, I think what you can do is extraordinary, like when you were sitting on the floor, legs spread eagle, and were able to get your entire chest on the floor."

"I learned that when I was studying at the Martha Graham School in New York. It's called second position."

"Well, I don't know what it's called, but to me it's first rate," he answered with a wink and a smile.

"I appreciate the compliment."

Alvin thought a moment and then said, "I think we could learn from each other. What if I took one of your classes? I'd be happy to help you in any way I can."

"Sounds like a good plan. I'm always willing to learn something new."

"So am I."

Chapter

9

Quickly, Susie's and Alvin's lives became deeply intertwined. Alvin invited her to go bike riding on their first date, and it was a memorable experience for both of them. Susie was delighted because Alvin took her on scenic routes that she hadn't known existed in Missouri. Alvin was impressed by Susie's stamina as she bicycled up high hills. But his admiration for her wasn't limited to her physical endurance— after she cooked him an exquisite dinner, it included her culinary expertise, as well.

As he entered her house that night with a bottle of wine under his arm, he was immediately greeted with the most delectable smells.

"Wow! What's cooking?" he asked. "Smells wonderful."

Susie opened the oven and showed him the salmon she was roasting with fresh herbs. "I also made a curried quinoa salad with apricots and almonds. As you can see, I'm into healthy eating."

"Great. So am I," he said. "And I'm starving."

"Good. We'll start with a salad of mixed greens, avocado, and dried cranberries. Hope you like them."

"Love them."

"Sometimes I like to indulge myself in a sinful dessert."

"Mmm, me too."

"So, I bought a chocolate mousse tart. Sound good?"

"Does it ever."

"Good, and I'm also glad you're famished."

Over dinner they shared personal stories of their childhoods, their similar tastes in music and current events, and their professional histories. Alvin sat back in his chair after dinner and exclaimed, "Wow, you're so talented! Not only a great teacher but also a great chef."

"Thanks so much," Susie replied. "I love to do both."

"Well, it shows."

Alvin and Susie's relationship swiftly deepened. Professionally, she taught him movements to make him more flexible, and he showed her new exercises for strength building. Personally, they discovered they shared many of the same passions, such as physical fitness, the arts, and fine cooking.

They often met at the gym and periodically watched each other's classes or training sessions. Due to her growing reputation, she was asked to teach more classes, including aerobics and Pilates sessions. She finally realized her dream when she opened her own studio as a Gyrotonic instructor. Alvin encouraged this venture, although he knew that as hard as she already worked, it would require even more time and energy to start a new business in addition to teaching and becoming certified in this new technique.

The Gyrotonic and Gyrokinesis Exercise System was a natural progression for Susie after all the dance, aerobics, and Pilates classes. It encompasses all of the various kinds of movement she had participated in from early childhood on, but it is even more focused and challenging. It includes movements found in swimming, yoga, gymnastics, dance, and tai chi, which were all familiar.

Susie was encouraged by her mentor, Tony Morales, a former dancer who had a Gyrotonic studio in New York. Tony was instrumental as her guide through the strenuous certification process. Susie's dad helped with the financing of the studio space, and her friend Ruthe Ponturo purchased the equipment in exchange for classes.

Only a little over a year after Susie started her business, the Gyrotonic studio was flourishing with clients. One of those clients was Susan Sherman, a beautiful, slim, active woman who bloomed in Susie's classes. The two Susans discovered that they had much more than their names in common.

"I can get you on a segment of one of the TV news programs," Susan excitedly announced one day.

"Really? How?"

"One of my friends is a newscaster, and I've been bragging about you and your classes. Honey, I want to make you and Gyrotonic famous."

The newscast was successful. As a result, Susie gained many more students, including the newscaster. Ultimately, many of her students became her friends, and her friends became her students.

Tony Morales had a similar experience with Susie. Tony had performed with major dance companies before he turned his efforts to Gyrotonic. He said that he felt a special bond with Susie as a teacher, student, and friend. Susie shared these feelings.

She scheduled many more trips to New York, not only because she was a New Yorker at heart but also because it gave her the opportunity to take advantage of Tony's expertise while completing the Gyrotonic certification process. This process would have been daunting for most people, but it invigorated Susie. She thrived on the challenge.

It was obvious how much she looked forward to classes with Tony. Sometimes I drove her into New York just to enjoy her company, and I found the smile on her face and her animation as she discussed Gyrotonic immensely gratifying. She would later emerge from one of these sessions red-faced and perspiring but sporting the most enormous, satisfied smile. Instruction by a master teacher augmented her passion for proper body-building exercise. It also seemed to touch her soul.

Tony asked Susie to participate in a demonstration video he was making. He had received a phone call from Jim Karas, a noted author, personal trainer, and TV exercise enthusiast with personal training studios located all over the country. Jim was well aware of Tony's reputation, and he also wanted to look at what was new and fun in fitness. Tony chose Susie to be his demonstrator in the video. Jim was astonished at Susie's strength and flexibility, and it was a rewarding experience for Susie to demonstrate what she believed in so strongly and to have the opportunity to share it with as many people as possible. Tony was delighted to host a nationally known exercise enthusiast at his studio and coordinate the program with a student such as Susie, who could demonstrate this technique to its best advantage.

Tony later said, "She was a tremendous presence. She was a joy to be around, totally honest, loved this work, and wanted to be the best teacher and student."

Tony combined his artistic endeavors by returning to his former career as a dancer and choreographer while still following his grueling Gyrotonic teaching schedule. His work was featured in two performances at the Manhattan Jewish Community Center in September 2011, and David, Rachel, and I attended opening night. It was a bittersweet event because I kept thinking about Susie and how much she would have loved and appreciated Tony's artistry, and how expertly he elicited quality performances from his dancers.

One of the works was titled "Life After Life." It was a moving solo work performed by a female dancer, which demonstrated the unfolding of the life of one human being with movements that covered the spectrum from vibrantly alive to lifeless. To me, it demonstrated that the spirit remains. The title made sense. After all, those we have loved live on in the survivors' minds and hearts. Rereading the title and the notes, I observed the following: "This piece is dedicated to the memory of Leni Wylliams [Tony's former teacher] and Susan Schaffer." I was speechless. Tony had simply and artfully captured the essence of his feelings for Susie.

I spoke to him after the performance and told him how touched we were.

"You know how much I admired her," he said.

Chapter

10

Eric and Susie had an enviable relationship. She was only four years older than her brother, but she became another mother to him from the moment he was born. She watched over him, insisting on helping me to bathe and diaper him. At four years of age, Susie was already showing signs of concern for others. She would rush in after school to play with and entertain her chubby baby brother. They made up Batman-and-Robin games. Susie was Robin and orchestrated the scenes, and although David and I could never determine whether she referred to Eric as "Bat Baby" or "Fat Baby," we always enjoyed watching their interactions.

When Susie was eight and Eric was four, we had the chance of a lifetime. David often traveled abroad on business, and there was an opportunity during a Christmas vacation for the entire family to go to Holland. The trip combined business and pleasure, and we visited a Dutch family that David knew. The Dutch family proved to be welcoming hosts who had a teenage son named Frank.

One day, while David was working, the Dutch family took Susie, Eric, and me to visit a typical Dutch home in Volendam, which was an island located outside of Amsterdam. Parking was not permitted near the homes, so we parked in a designated area close to the ocean.

As a four-year-old, Eric was uninterested, but his big sister tried to convince him that this was worth seeing. She told him they would do something else that was fun for him afterward, and besides, he would see Daddy later. Nothing doing. The walk from the car to the house was too long and boring as far as Eric was concerned. His patience wore thin while the elderly Dutch guide showed all the visitors the typical Dutch home.

"I'm leaving," he announced.

Susie whispered, "Just be patient. The tour will be over soon."

The tour ended soon after that, and we all looked around, but Eric was nowhere to be found. Susie ran out of the house with Frank, the Dutch couple's teenage son, following her. It was December and the middle of winter, cold and damp, especially since this tourist site faced the ocean.

"Eric!" she yelled.

No answer.

"Eric!" she yelled even louder, as Frank yelled along with her.

"Please don't worry," he said. "We'll find him. He couldn't have gone very far."

"But he's my little brother, and he could have done anything. Maybe he jumped into the water."

"No chance," said Frank. "He's too smart. and he knows the water is freezing. Let's walk back to the car. Maybe he walked back."

Everyone ran toward the car while Susie cried frantically. Between hysterical sobs, she was shrieking.

"If I don't find him there, I'm going to say the worst curse word I know—dammit, dammit, dammit!"

Then Susie let out an ear-piercing scream. Miraculously, her little brother was standing by the car. She ran over and hugged Eric as hard as she could, laughing and crying at the same time.

"What's wrong?"

"I thought you were lost."

"No, I was right here," he said. "I knew where I was going."

"But I didn't!"

Though there was a normal amount of sibling rivalry, Susie and Eric were always supportive of each other as children and teenagers. Susie was always there for her brother. This was clear during a particular incident when Eric was in junior high and Susie in high school. During one of her classes, Susie received a note from the principal to come quickly to the nurse's office because Eric had an accident. She hurried and found Eric looking pale and in obvious pain, with the school nurse holding both of his wrists.

Both children were in tears: Eric because he was in pain, and Susie because she was upset to see him in pain. "Have you called my mother?" she quickly asked the nurse.

When I arrived, the nurse told me she was touched to see how the big sister took care of her younger brother. She said that Susie had run into the room and then kept hugging and stroking Eric.

My arrival initiated further tears, mostly from Susie.

"Don't cry, Susie," Eric said as the three of us drove to the doctor's office. "It was stupid of me." Susie kept cuddling him.

Later, the story came out. It seems that Eric was showing off his athletic prowess and twirling on two metal bars. He saw that he was going too fast, tried to stop himself by jumping off, and landed on the cement sidewalk on both wrists. The x-rays confirmed two broken wrists. Susie was even more tender toward her brother during the weeks he recovered.

Growing up, the two of them shared a love of sports, especially football and their favorite team, the New York Giants. David bought season tickets. From the time Susie was six years old, and as Eric grew, the three of them would talk incessantly about the game they had seen the previous week and their expectations for the following week. As adults, Susie and Eric fondly recalled going to the Super Bowl in Florida with my husband. It was a memorable experience for the three of them, even though their beloved team lost; what was most important was that they were together.

David reserved two hotel rooms for the three of them, thinking that he and Eric would share a room and Susie would have a single. Much to my husband's amazement, Susie and Eric wanted to share a room so they could talk. "Dad," they said, "we don't really get much of a chance to be together and this is what we want."

David liked to tell a story about Susie when she was six years old and already a rabid Giants fan. The Giants were playing badly and losing the game. This innocent-looking child stood up in her seat, raised her arm, and screamed at the top of her lungs, "You suck!"

Susie's visits from St. Louis to New York always included time alone with her brother so they could catch up on their lives. She always visited Eric at his office in Manhattan following one of her classes with Tony Morales. Eric said he was thrilled to show off his sister. "She was fun, smart, and beautiful," he recalled. When she opened the Gyrotonic studio, Eric was not only proud of her accomplishment but eager to hear about her new venture as a businesswoman.

But then, in one instant, their close relationship was cruelly severed. Eric told me that for many months after Susie's murder, when someone said to him, "Have a nice day," he would think to himself, "To hell with you. How could it ever be nice? My sister's dead."

Chapter

11

Susie demonstrated unusual maturity on the one hand, but, on the other, she could be a typical teenager. Some of the things she did were worrisome and scary. I liked to tell her she was a peach but became a pit when she got herself into trouble.

Her mothering instincts were very strong. Those instincts included looking me over whenever I dressed to go out. I was her mother, but often she would mother me. I loved it. She had a flair for coordinating an outfit, and she would run to my closet, choose a scarf, and drape it on me, saying, "Mommy, you need something to tie that outfit together better." It always turned out to be just the right accessory.

She demonstrated her caring nature in so many other ways. When Susie was in her third year at Skidmore College in Saratoga Springs, New York, I was getting a new car and gave her the one I was currently driving. The plan was for me to drive with her and all of her belongings to Saratoga Springs just before school started. I was then going to return home by bus to the New York Port Authority Terminal and David would meet me there.

I helped her unpack and set her room up, and the time came for me to return home. "Ma," Susie asked, "do you have a book to read? It's a long ride."

"Sure," I answered. "You know I always remember to bring a book."

Susie took me to the bus stop, walked me onto the bus, and sat me down in the front seat. "Now," she said, "open up your book, do not look to the right or the left, and do not talk to anyone, because a lot of seedy-looking people travel on this bus." I couldn't resist answering her by quoting the title of the book *Are You My Mother?* which Susie loved to hear me read to her when she was a child. I laughed to myself on the bus ride home. Susie could be a troublesome teenager, but she could also be a protective little old lady.

Because she was human and a teenager, she got into varying degrees of trouble. There was the time she played hooky during her junior year of high school with her friend Dara Levine. Susie and Dara were both good students, but they had a propensity for living a little on the edge. They left school on this particular day to travel by train into Manhattan and returned home as they normally would after a day at school. The school called our home the next day to check on Susie's absence.

"Where were you?" I asked when Susie returned from school that afternoon. She turned beet red, hesitated for just a moment, and then poured out the events of her and Dara's escapade.

"OK, Ma," she said, "this is the story: Dara and I wanted to visit a friend we knew at her private school in the city. We sat in on one of her classes, and you know what?"

"I'm all ears."

"That private school is much stricter than our public school."

Susie took a breath and continued. "I have to tell you the best part. I knew I was doing wrong by cutting school, but we got the thrill of our lives."

"How's that?" I answered, somewhat annoyed but ready to listen.

Susie blurted out, "We saw John Lennon and Yoko Ono and got their autographs!"

I stopped for a moment to process this information. I had very mixed emotions, not knowing whether to punish her or laugh and share the joy she felt. My reaction was to do both. I told her it was wrong and she knew it but expressed my delight in their extemporaneous meeting. She knew she had done wrong and was honest about it. Secretly, I was a little envious. It was a great sharing experience that I will always remember.

Another time, Susie got in trouble by talking back to one of her teachers in high school. This particular teacher had a hard and fast rule that demanded punctuality. If students were not present by 8:00 a.m. precisely, they would not be allowed in class that day, in addition to receiving a demerit.

Susie was punctual to a fault. However, on this day she was delayed. She arrived four minutes after the hour, and the door was shut in her face. She begged the teacher to allow her to come in, but he was unrelenting. Finally, Susie lost her cool, erupting into a loud barrage of abusive expressions directed at the teacher.

I received a phone call during the day from this teacher, who related the incident to me. I questioned Susie when she arrived home that afternoon.

"Ma, he's an asshole," she replied.

"That's not nice."

"I know," she said, "but he's unfair."

"Just tell me what happened."

"First," Susie said, "you know I always make it my business to be on time. But this time, I needed to go to the bathroom and was embarrassed to tell him."

"I understand, but you weren't right in cursing at him either."

"Yes, I know, but my mouth got the better of me," she said.

"Listen, honey, as long as you know your reaction wasn't right, either. So the question is: What are you going to do about it?"

"Hmm, I think I'll apologize for what I said, not what I did, because that teacher is a hard-nose."

"Good idea. You'll be the better person for doing it."

Susie got an A in that course, but an F in conduct.

Then there was the matter of the tattoo she got during a summer's dance residency at Reed College in Oregon, which concentrated on the Graham technique. The course was taught by Armgard von Bardeleben, a favorite teacher of Susie's whom she admired professionally and personally.

Armgard was a no-nonsense person. Everyone looked up to her both figuratively and literally because she was over six feet tall. Her striking presence, combined with her energy and sense of logic, resonated with all of her students, including Susie.

It was a joy to hear the stories Susie related when she returned home after completing the summer course. During one of our many talks, as she changed clothes, I suddenly noticed a Band-aid placed just underneath her buttocks.

"Did you cut yourself?" I asked.

With a half-smile, she said, "No, Ma, it's a tattoo." She removed the Band-aid, revealing a small lotus flower.

Though I was initially taken aback, I will admit that the tattoo was neatly and artfully executed. She showed her usual good taste in spite of the negative connotations I associated with tattoos. My perception was that only sailors or "dese, dem, and dose" guys got tattoos. I quickly decided to play it cool and not get excited as she showed me her new body ornament.

"Hmm, it's pretty and not intrusive," I said. "I just hope it didn't hurt during the process and you aren't in any discomfort now."

"No, Ma. It's fine, and thanks for not going crazy."

"What good would it have done me? You did it. I'm just curious. Did Armgard see it?"

"Yeah."

"What was her reaction?"

"I know she wasn't pleased. But like you accepted it, so did she, because she knew there was nothing she could do about it."

Susie regretted getting the tattoo as she grew into adulthood.

I saw Armgard after Susie died. She recalled the tattoo and how she had disapproved. "She could be a tough teenager," Armgard remarked. She told me how much she had enjoyed having Susie as a student, stressing her willingness to work hard and improve her skills in the Graham technique. Armgard said she was pleased that Susie had completed her Gyrotonic certification. "She put her vitality and training to good use," she added. "I had hoped to tell her that personally one day."

"You were her role model," I answered. Regrettably, in January 2012 Susie's beloved teacher and friend Armgard also died.

The "scary" instances included using controlled substances. One day, when Susie was about fifteen years old, I was looking at her and realized something was wrong. "You look tired to me," I said. "Do you feel all right?"

"Sure, Ma."

"Then why do you look so tired and flushed? Your eyes are droopy, like you have a fever."

"I'm stoned."

"You're what?" I said, astounded.

"Stoned, high on marijuana," Susie said more emphatically.

I was rendered mute. It took a few minutes to regain my powers of speech. Then I reminded her that she must know about the dangers of using controlled substances. Her response was, "I know it, Ma, but don't cha know it's just a phase I'm going through?" At first, her remark seemed flippant. My brain quickly processed it and concluded that if nothing else, Susie was always honest, even when she knew she was doing wrong. Also, I knew she was aware of the pitfalls but was experimenting like a typical teenager. I discussed this incident with David later that evening, and we both agreed that my reaction was cool but correct.

Still, she was prone to experimenting with controlled substances. When Susie was sixteen, she tried a minuscule amount of LSD, and this was even more upsetting.

David and I returned home after doing errands one Saturday afternoon. Susie seemed agitated and was pacing back and forth from one room to the next. She stopped for a moment and burst into tears.

"What's wrong?" I asked her as we both hugged her and tried to comfort her and calm her down.

"If I tell you something bad that I did, will you still love me?" She was breathing deeply, tears kept falling, and her nose was running.

I handed her a tissue. "Of course we will, and we do." We were still hugging Susie as hard as we could. "You just have to tell us what has you so upset so that we can help you."

"Mommy, Daddy, Mommy, Daddy," she kept repeating. "I'm so scared. I'm so scared . . . and I'll never do it again."

"Susie, darling, what are you talking about? Never do what again?" I asked.

"Take LSD," she whispered.

David and I looked at one another. I could see him wince, and the pit of my stomach felt uneasy.

"Where did you get it?"

"From the older brother of one of the girls in school. He dared me to take it . . . and I did." She was still crying uncontrollably. "It was such a small amount, no more than like a pinch from a baby aspirin."

David and I looked at one another. "I think we need to call her doctor," David said.

The doctor told us to put her to bed. "Let her sleep it off. Then call me, and I'll see you in my office."

Susie slept for several hours. We called the doctor when she awoke, and we met him in his office later that afternoon. He asked Susie why she did it.

"Because it was there. I didn't think I would have such a trip."

"It's a very strong substance, Susie," he said quietly.

"I know. I guess I'm not perfect," she answered.

"None of us is," the three of us said almost in unison. The doctor added, "We're human, and as humans we do things we know we shouldn't."

The three of us listened, acutely aware of the doctor's sensitivity and thoughtful choice of words. "You're lucky you have understanding parents and that they arrived home when they did."

A noticeable shiver passed through her body, and her eyes started to water again. "I know," she said.

"The main thing you have to remember is that this is a critical lesson you have learned, and not do it again."

Susie said, "You can bet I won't."

David and I tried to reassure each other during such hair-raising times that the real, caring, cooperative Susie would emerge eventually and remain, which she did. Taking drugs and getting the tattoo made Susie intensely aware as an adult and mother. I once heard her speaking to her children, telling them in no uncertain terms about the dangers of taking any controlled substances. She said, "I speak from experience and know the telltale signs. So you can't pull anything like that on me. I was there. I did it, and I'm telling you because it's no fun and most of all because I love you."

Chapter

12

"He's mine, not yours."

That is how Susie referred to my husband David when she was four. He was her daddy. For the first four years of Susie's life, she was an only child and as such received unlimited attention. Between hugs and kisses, this occasional remark—"He's mine, not yours"— indicated the relationship between Susie and my husband when we were together as a family. I enjoyed it when she threw her arms around him and said those words.

Once, after I repeated this phrase she used, I was asked whether I was jealous due to Susie's possessive attitude toward her father. It was an interesting question, but I didn't have to think about my response. I said I felt very secure in the knowledge that Susie loved me. She had me all the time, but she didn't have David because he traveled on business a great deal during her formative first years. He always devoted quality time to his daughter whenever he was home. That was when Susie made up for the lost time when he wasn't there. I always thought it was adorable and funny, and sometimes it was even funnier.

Susie was precocious at eighteen months but not toilet trained. When she needed to be changed, she would clearly announce, "I have a dirty diaper." I was a full-time mother and usually changed her diaper. When David arrived home after traveling abroad, exhausted and jet-lagged, I volunteered to do the "dirty work."

Susie's pronouncement was, "Only my daddy will do it." David would smile graciously and without hesitation say, "Come on, Susie, let's get you changed." I knew Susie missed him during those long business trips and wanted his full attention. Having him change her diaper was one way of doing it.

Aside from being verbally precocious as a youngster, Susie was observant and frequently described in detail what she noticed. For example, she would say to me, "When my daddy comes home, I'm going to take off his hat, give him a hug and a kiss, and say, 'Hi, honey, how are you?'" This was exactly what I did whenever David arrived home either from a day at the office or a long business trip abroad.

Susie viewed her daddy as a softie as she was growing up, particularly when she was a teenager. Sometimes she asked David for permission to do something that I had already said no to. She wasn't unique in this respect. David, of course, was on to her and would relate the conversation to me later. He would say, "Did you ask your mother?"

"Yes," she would say, usually red-faced.

"And what was her answer?"

Though David was typically a softie, Susie would realize she had been outdone and knew better than to respond to David or pursue it any further.

The affection Susie and her father felt for each other grew even stronger as she matured and had children of her own. The following anecdotes illustrate their loving but quirky relationship.

David awoke early every morning to work out at the gym located in his office building. He arrived equipped with his clothes so he could shower and dress there after he had finished exercising.

One particular morning, he sent an e-mail to Susie and Rachel that read: "When I was getting ready to leave, I saw my watch on the night table. After putting on my workout clothes, I reached for it to take it with me, but it was gone. I looked all over for it for several minutes, and then left in frustration, knowing, however, that my good wife would find it eventually. When I got to the office to work out, I found it—on my wrist."

Susie responded: "Dad, it's like the time I couldn't find my cell phone anywhere, called it from the house phone, and realized it was in my hand. This is one of the reasons why I love you so much. I'm glad that I'm just like you and just as forgetful."

Rachel also responded with an e-mail to her mom and grand-father: "Ditto what Mom said. This among countless other reasons is why I also love you both so much. Next time someone asks me why I'm so forgetful, I will show them this e-mail and tell them that it's in my blood."

Susie grew up respecting her father as a role model in his legal profession and athletics. She inherited his love for sports—the Giants, tennis, and running. She ran marathons, just like her dad. However, she also watched out for him. Sometimes, Susie admonished him for pushing himself too far. This was further demonstration of the concern she showed others and especially her dad.

She was a mature woman and a mother when she told him in no uncertain terms, "Dad, I know how much you love to run, but there's something called too much. Even the best athletes take a day off to rest their bodies. You need to do that. Your body needs one day of rest. The words are to do 'zip, zero, zilch.'"

Susie was thrilled when her dad ran the New York marathon four times. The last time, she became worried when he didn't appear at the finishing pathway in Central Park when she expected him. "What if he's lying in the street and we don't know it?" she exclaimed. Her protective, little-old-lady persona became full-blown, just like her reaction when she put me on the bus to the Port Authority. I remained calm and tried to reassure her by reasoning that there were many runners and it took time for each one to get through all of the check-in paperwork. She immediately ran to make several purchases at one of the food concessions in the park and showed up a few minutes later with nuts, raisins, and energy bars. "He'll need protein and energy," she said. This was typical of Susie's caring nature. It made her feel that she was doing something to help someone she loved, while also taking her mind off her fears.

We both supported her in various ways through her contentious divorce and exercise training, but it was her father she looked to for expertise in legal and business advice. Susie's success as a businesswoman in the field she loved was a product of their coordinated efforts.

David and I never acknowledged Mother's or Father's Day. We have always regarded them as too commercial. However, on Father's Day only six months before Susie died, she said she had found the perfect Father's Day card, the quintessential expression of their relationship. There's a drawing of a girl on the front of the card and the caption reads, "You're the kind of dad most people wish they had." On the inside it reads, "Glad you're mine. Happy Father's Day." Susie included the following statement: "Not that I need this commercial day to tell you—but I do want you to know that I feel very blessed every day of my life to have you as my dad—All my love, Susie."

Chapter

13

David and I were talking to Susie one day in the spring of 2007. She told us that she and Eric were talking about our fiftieth wedding anniversary coming up in June. "You should have a celebration. Eric agrees, and we want to organize it. Whadda ya think?"

"Hmm, nice idea," I said, "and so sweet of you and Eric to think of it."

"Mom and Dad," she answered, "you know what you always say, grab the good stuff, because to use your expression, 'Shit happens.'"

"We'll talk about it and get back to you."

"You have so many friends who would love celebrating with you."

Our fiftieth wedding anniversary celebration did take place. We will always remember it because it was a special time surrounded by our children, who coordinated all the details. In attendance were other family and meaningful friends, many of whom we'd known since childhood.

The most memorable incident occurred when Eric and Susie spoke to our guests. Susie said:

My grandma was the worrier (now it's me) but truly my dad is a quiet worrier—though he may not admit it. My mother is one in a billion—there isn't anything she wouldn't do—even for a stranger on the street (no exaggeration). It used to be embarrassing to me how effusive she is—but now I realize that I'm like that. I love and understand her personality and realize I'm just like her in many ways.

As different as my mom and dad seem on the outside, they really share so many things, things that are the foundation of a successful long-term marriage such as theirs. Probably the one thing that makes their marriage one that has 'super-power' strength is that they survived raising *me*. Some of you know I was, shall we say, a challenge to raise, but truly they showed me only unconditional love, a united front, and kept telling me I was OK. The support my parents give not only to Eric and me but to my children and his children is so special. They derive so much joy from spending time traveling for and with their grandchildren.

I can't make it any clearer, Mom and Dad. We all love you and are so glad that we pulled off this party because it gives us pleasure the way you have given it to us.

"Grabbing the good stuff" became an even more meaningful expression because eighteen months later Susie was dead.

Chapter

14

"I can't wait to tell you what Rachel said yesterday. My sweet little three-year-old daughter."

Susie had stopped by our house after teaching an exercise class and before she had to pick Rachel up at her nursery school. The expression on Susie's face was a mixture of surprise and enjoyment with just a hint of disapproval.

"So, what did she say?" I asked.

"Asshole."

"What?" I was taken aback but thought it was funny.

"Yes, you heard me. Out of the mouths of babes."

"But why?" I asked, and both of us chuckled.

"This is the story. Yesterday, I had to make a quick stop at the supermarket and saw that I still had time left on the meter. It took me a little longer than I thought. I came out carrying Rachel and the few things I bought just as the meter expired, and there was a policeman already writing me a ticket."

"That's frustrating, and it can't be undone once he starts writing the ticket."

"Tell me about it. I was annoyed and tried to reason with the policeman, to no avail. It was too late. Rachel saw that I was annoyed, and as I was putting her into her car seat she said, "Was that person an asshole?"

"Hmm, she comes by it honestly. Did you say anything to her?"

"I told her I know she's heard me say bad words and that was a bad word. I said I would try not to say anything like that again and neither should she."

"Rachel is smart and observant just like you were. She hears things and repeats them just like you did." I couldn't help but recall Susie watching guys playing basketball in the park and hearing gutter language that must have made an impression on her. There was also the time when she was almost four and we were driving to visit my parents. She was already reading at this age. David stopped at a red light, and Susie noticed large letters written on the bark of a tree. First, she spelled out the letters "S-H-I-T," continually repeating them. Then she said the actual word over and over, clearly liking the sound of it. David and I couldn't believe what we were hearing.

"Shit, shit, shit! What does it mean?" she asked innocently.

David and I tried to be serious, but we were overcome with the giggles. "Not a nice word," David managed to answer between fits of laughter that made his eyes tear. Quickly, he changed the subject to the fun we were going to have when we arrived at her grandparents' house.

Rachel was and is a duplicate of Susie in many ways. As children, they were both perceptive and precocious. As adults, they shared the same feelings about concern for others and doing the right thing.

Like Susie, Rachel was disappointed in Peter's actions.

Rachel was the only child for five years until the birth of her brother Daniel, which was followed by an immediate and soon-to-be traumatic move to St. Louis. Within three years Sarah was born, and Susie and Peter were getting divorced.

Rachel felt the brunt of it. First she had a devoted father, and then things were completely reversed. Although her life was turned upside down, she was always sure of the unconditional love and support her mother showed her all through her teenage years, in startling contrast to her father's indifference. As a teenager, Rachel understood that Susie had the strength and character to maintain her equilibrium as a single mother and a working woman.

Just after Susie died, her reincarnation in Rachel was exquisitely demonstrated in two incidents during an observance of Yom Kippur. David has always fasted on this solemn day. He also runs every morning and, as always, was going to run this morning as well as fast. Rachel learned of his plan and admonished him. "Poppy," she said, "it's not healthy. You shouldn't do it."

"I do it every day," he answered, "and I've done it on Yom Kippur for many years."

"Poppy, at least you eat after you run every day, and besides, you're getting older and should take extra care and not do it on Yom Kippur if you're going to fast."

Rachel received a phone call from her father on this sad day just after we returned from the memorial service at our temple. He was completely oblivious as to the significance of this day.

"So, how was your day?"

"Sad."

"Why?" he asked.

We watched Rachel grimace, but she responded in a mature manner that made us proud. "Dad," she said, "it's Yom Kippur, and if you don't know what it means, I suggest you Google it."

The concern Rachel showed her "Poppy" about his exercising and the response to her father were indicative of our daughter's teaching, the caring nature she had instilled in Rachel, and the respect they both had for their heritage. It is all bittersweet. Susie lives.

Chapter

15

Daniel was Susie's "little man." He was not as verbal as Rachel had been at his age, but he was a cuddler. In our many conversations from St. Louis to New York, Susie always told me how this chubby little boy loved to cuddle with her and would try to do it as often as he could. She welcomed every opportunity to hug and kiss him.

Susie told me that Daniel was attracted to all the toys that interest boys: airplanes, cars, trucks, fire engines, and guns. The guns were the only thing that Susie unconditionally rejected, even water guns. I once heard her say to him, "It's fine to make believe you're driving a car or a truck, but even to make believe you're shooting someone is not."

From the time Daniel was three, Susie often told me about her recurrent arguments with him when it came to playing with a gun of any kind. She always said, "There's too much violence out there, and I don't like my son even playing at it."

Susie was always a source of support for Daniel as he grew up. He was deeply affected by his parents' divorce, but his mother was his pillar of strength. Even as a little boy, he noticed that his father was attentive only to him and not to his sisters. It bothered him, but he was not able to verbalize his concern to his mother. Susie told me that when Daniel was about nine, he was finally able to question her about it.

"What did you say?" I asked.

"I told him I was proud of him for being so observant and glad he was able to talk about it with me."

"Good for you. Anything else?"

"Yes, I told him that I've spoken to Peter about the neglectful way he treats the girls, but it doesn't seem to help."

"What did he say to that?"

"'It's not right.'"

"He's very sensitive. How did you respond to that?"

"I said he and I knew it isn't right, but it served no purpose to dwell on it. The main thing is that I was proud of him for his perception and the fact that he was able to talk to me about it."

"Good answer, Susie."

Susie told me that Daniel often turned to her for advice about his social life, and he was always comforted by her honest, thoughtful counseling. At one point, a girlfriend had been giving him a hard time.

"I asked him what the problem was with this girl."

"What *was* the problem?" I asked.

"He went on and on. He told me she was constantly calling, e-mailing, and texting him and that it was too much. She keeps asking him whether he loves her. He has a life and doesn't want to be choked by her continually bothering him."

"What was your response?"

"I told him he had to make it clear to her how he feels, but in a nice way. Of course, I think she has good taste, but that's beside the point. That he had to find a way to tell her kindly that they're only seventeen and it's better for her as well as for him to attend to other things in their lives."

"What did he say?"

"He said, 'You're the best.'"

David and I often wonder what Daniel is thinking now that his confidante is dead. He does not bare his innermost feelings, at least not to us. In those four years, Daniel has graduated from college. If Susie were alive, he would have continued to share his thoughts about all aspects of his life. His respect for his mother's opinion was important to him. Our hope is that he will find a meaningful source to express his emotions and future plans.

Chapter

16

All of Susie's children are interesting, and each is special in his or her own way. Rachel was reserved throughout her teenage years and grew into a mature young woman. Daniel was always a calm young man of few words, except on the occasions when he looked to his mother for good, honest advice. Sarah is a typical teenager, sweet, fun-loving, needing to stand up for herself because of her father's neglect, and with a temper that can erupt when she doesn't get her way.

I frequently received phone calls from Susie when she needed to vent about Sarah's various outbursts. "On the one hand, she can be terrific. On the other, she can drive me crazy. I guess she's just being hormonal."

"What happened?"

"Well, Ma, she got angry with me when I told her I didn't want her to go to a concert on a school night. Wow, did she curse me out! This was last night and I'm still shaking."

"I know what you mean. Good for you for sticking to your principles."

"I try to. She's only fifteen but thinks she can do whatever she wants. I tried to remain calm while she was ranting and slamming doors. Whew! I'm exhausted from hearing her screams and hot temper. All I kept thinking is that it would've been wonderful to put her in deep freeze."

"I don't blame you."

"Mom, you should've heard her. 'I hate you, I hate you, I hate you!' I couldn't resist saying that I loved her over and over again and that was why I didn't want her to go."

"You know I've always told you that we lash out at the people we love most. She loves you, so it's easy for her to give you lip."

"I know that, and that's what Alvin says, too. He's great. Most of the time, he can calm Sarah down, but there's a difference. I know I was sometimes impossible as a teenager, but you and Daddy were united. As great as Alvin is, he's not her father, and he makes it a practice not to butt in. My ex-husband is either nowhere to be found or a hindrance."

"Too bad. He's missing out on a great kid."

"I know it," Susie said.

"So how was Sarah this morning?"

"She came down from her bedroom before going to school with a smile on her face and gave me a big hug and a kiss."

"There you go."

Sarah wrote a gut-wrenching piece two months after her mother's death. She expressed in minute detail her innermost feelings and how those feelings seemed to envelop her like a second skin. She wrote:

> *I don't understand life. I don't understand why bad*
> *things happen to good people. Why is the world such*
> *a hurtful place? I don't understand why someone so*
> *beautiful and amazing and intelligent and inspiring*
> *and loving and caring would be murdered. Why do*
> *such things happen? All I know is that every day I*

feel happy, sad, hurt, pain, laughter, and grateful all in one. I don't know how to juggle all of these emotions. Am I doing it right? What is the best thing to do? Talk about what happened and how much I miss my mom? Or just do what I have been doing and put on a happy face and try to live my life? It's so hard because I WANT to be happy, but after everything that has happened to me it makes wanting to be happy less important. I NEED to be sad. It feels good to cry. I want to feel the agony and pain I'm in. I hate not being sad, but I also hate being sad. I love being happy, but what is there to be happy about? I'm happy I have amazing friends. I'm happy I have an amazing family but I'm scared to death they won't be around. I'm so scared to lose someone else. I couldn't take it. I'm having such a hard time. I don't have a mom. Every time I see a mom it reminds me that I don't have one anymore. She was taken from me. And that hurts so badly. Why do innocent people get killed? I hate this world but I also can't imagine anything else than what this world is. It seems like a fantasy world where there is no crime and everyone is happy. That would be awesome. But that's just fantasy. I miss my old life and I'm so mad at myself for taking it for granted. I miss living in my cluttered house with Alvin and my mom and brother. I miss watching my mom do her ridiculous exercise routines. I miss my mom's food. I'm in so much pain now that's she's gone. Why was it her? I still can't believe it. I would give up everything just to have her back. I wish there was a way I could go back in time and change everything that happened December 16. I would have come straight home from school and answered the door so they wouldn't have burglarized my house. I wish I could change everything. I wish it had been me who found her, not my brother. He didn't deserve that. None of us deserved what happened to us. What was the reason? Everything happens for a reason, so what? I still don't know what I did so bad to deserve this. My mom was an amazing person who loved life. Why was her life taken? She had so much more to do and experience. She came to my room crying because she was happy Obama got elected. Now she doesn't even get to experience him as president. I swear one day Gyrotonic will be huge and that would have been my mom leading the crowd. She won't be at my siblings' weddings or mine or be a grandmother. She won't even know our spouses. That is so screwed up. Her kids were taken from her. The people she loved the most; she's not here with them. Where is she? Is she gone? Is there a heaven? I just don't know. All I know is that I hope someday I will be with her again. If there was solid proof that there is a heaven and everyone that dies before you is waiting for you to come, I would have killed myself December 16. That sounds bad but it's true. She's been and still is the most important person to me. She gave me life. And I took her for granted. I would kill to have another stupid argument with her, or have her kiss me on the cheek. I wish she could give me some sign that she's still watching over me. Words can't describe how much I miss her and want her back. I still can't believe this happened, that this is actually my life.

I mean I know it is, but it still feels like yesterday I was coming home from school to my house on Nimes Drive.

Chapter
17

Julie and Susie first met when their two daughters were in the same class in the first grade. Sarah was Susie's third child and Danielle was Julie's fourth. The girls were the initial link, but the bond became infinitely greater over time. The two young girls became thick as thieves, and the two mothers were similarly drawn to each other. Susie and Julie shared many values as mothers and as people committed to helping others. It was also nice that their August birthdays were three days apart.

Julie told us about their connection and how it deepened over the years.

"We considered ourselves soul sisters and could talk for hours. It began with our two headstrong daughters. They had minds of their own and drove us to distraction with things like the endless phone calls Sarah and Danielle had when they wanted to go to a late-night concert on a school night. All hell broke loose in both of our homes, but we stayed strong and supported each other. We gave our daughters the same reasons we couldn't give our permission to go. Over a weekend it would've been fine, but this was a school night. Staying up too late would be bad for their health, as well as their schoolwork."

Julie said that she and Susie would share silly questions like, "When do you think they should start shaving?" or "Is it too early to let them get their ears pierced?"

They shared their commitment to family and Judaism and spent many of the Jewish holidays together and with Alvin's family. They both appreciated fine food and good cooking. Susie's and Julie's passion for keeping fit and exercising meshed, and Julie was one of Susie's supporters when she opened her Gyrotonic studio. They shared intimate secrets. Julie said, "We would share the truth even when it hurt. If she happened to be down, I could lift her spirits, and vice-versa. We had a way of bringing out the best in one another. We also allowed space for each of us to shine and grow. We felt electrifying energy when we were around each other."

It was sadly ironic when Julie said, "We shared our daughters. I trusted and respected her so much that I asked her to finish raising my daughter if anything ever happened to me."

Julie continues to share her innermost thoughts with me about the cherished friendship she had with Susie. "We have a different relationship now. We're not able to have a physical one, but we have an extremely strong spiritual one. I dream about it and feel from my dreams that she's at peace. There isn't a day that goes by that I don't look at her picture and tell her how much I miss her and love her. I miss her energy, uniqueness, inner and outer beauty, amazing hugs, and our closeness."

Julie called me one day because she had found a quote in a drawer that was characteristic of their relationship. She said, "I must have cut it out from some magazine right after Susie died and put it away because it was too painful to read then, but I want to read it to you now because it speaks directly to how we felt about each other." Her voice trembled as she began to read: "Invite people into your life who will circle you with love. Their friendship will be like water to your soul. They will see you're good even when you don't. When you look into their eyes and into their heart, you see yourself at your best."

My connection with Julie remains important in keeping Susie's memory alive. She was Susie's friend and now she is my friend. It's like when a link has been removed in a bracelet. The connection is strengthened by tightening what remains, and we are the remaining links.

Chapter

18

Ruthe Ponturo followed Susie from the time she taught Pilates classes, and their relationship deepened as time went on. Ruthe discovered Gyrotonic on a trip to California. She told Susie about the exercise system, and Susie said that she had also heard about it and was going to do some investigating. It was Ruthe who helped Susie start her career in Gyrotonic by purchasing all the necessary equipment in exchange for classes. Their friendship was also based on their shared love for the arts, the Democratic Party, Barack Obama's imminent campaign, and good food.

Their connection was further cemented after Susie learned that she was chosen to discuss the Gyrotonic system on a television news segment. She chose Ruthe to demonstrate the exercises on the equipment while she described the fine points of the technique. It was an exciting experience for both of them to be on a major television station and share the benefits of the technique.

Susie and Ruthe affectionately shared their feelings with me about each other at varying times. Susie told me how much she loved Ruthe for her warmth, appreciation of her teaching, and interest Ruthe showed in her personal life. "She was a great student and great friend," Susie said. "Ruthe was always eager to share her experience in taking my class. She only wanted to tell the world about Gyrotonic for everyone's benefit health-wise, as well as mine financially."

Ruthe was always ready to listen to Susie and lend support during her divorce, and she was sympathetic about the effect it had on the children. Ruthe told me how much she admired Susie. "She was so much fun, with a strong character. In spite of her personal difficulties, she was a role model for other women who had to endure the same circumstances. She always had a smile on her face and a positive attitude."

Ruthe occasionally traveled to New York and sometimes her visits coincided with Susie's. It was a pleasure to see Susie's excitement when she and Ruthe were in New York at the same time. Their visits were further enhanced when they could both take a class with Tony Morales and enjoy Manhattan together.

Ruthe now lives in New York and is a student at Tony's Gyrotonic studio. She told me, "Tony and I always talk about her."

Chapter

19

Mark Shapiro, a man in his fifties, was a friend of Ruthe's. He was a gentle, clever, and articulate person with a keen sense of humor. He was heftily built, and it seemed incongruous for him to connect with Gyrotonic or anything to do with dance. But he did. He became a student of Susie's after Ruthe jokingly challenged Mark to try taking a Gyrotonic class. Mark accepted the challenge. He said he ultimately fell in love with the program and the instructor.

Susie often spoke about Mark to me. She told me he was amazed by his progress in this form of exercise within a short period of time. Though it was a challenge for him, his proficiency increased through Susie's encouragement and his own feelings of success. Mark told me that he regarded Susie as an inspirational teacher, which was an important element in strengthening his relationship with her as both client and friend.

They had two other commonalities: politics and music. Like Ruthe's relationship with Susie regarding their similar political values, Mark and Susie's connection was also fostered by Barack Obama's 2008 presidential candidacy. Discussions were always part of their training sessions, as were e-mails regarding his commitment to Obama, which he shared with Susie. They also spoke about their love for music during Gyrotonic sessions. They had similar eclectic tastes; their mutual love for classics, folk, and pop tunes enhanced their alliance. Susie often told me that Mark would download a CD and bring it each time he came to class. Sharing music this way became a ritual. Many of the songs he brought were those she fondly remembered from her formative years.

"Ma, he's such a nice person," she said during one of our telephone conversations.

"Sounds like it. Clearly, it's his way to express his gratitude to you for adding another dimension to his life."

David and I continued to communicate with Mark after Susie died. Just like the rest of us, Mark had to find ways to function without his dear friend, support system, and teacher. "She was such a vital force and someone I depended on for so many reasons," he told me. I spoke to him at one point about my concerns regarding illegal handgun possession, which we agreed was a cause that required never-ending persistence. I also told him how ironic it was that Susie was always against gun possession and wouldn't even allow Daniel to play with a water gun. He and I discussed the means of raising people's consciousness about this issue while paying tribute to Susie.

Mark called me one day. "Lois, I'm writing a script for a documentary. That's how I want to honor Susie, and I think I know people who can help me get it produced."

"That's a great idea. It seems like we're both on the same track. I also wrote a draft for a documentary," I said. "But now I've begun to write a book that basically focuses on two main issues."

"What are they?"

"I want to tell my personal story about all of the aspects of Susie's life as a child, adult, and mother, including her work, and ultimately use it as a vehicle to stir up concern and action against illegal handgun possession."

"Sounds interesting, Lois."

"I hope so. Tragedies like ours happen every day, and I want to put a face on it with someone a reader can relate to."

"Lois, this is an excellent idea. It takes a lot of courage to attempt a project like that. I'm proud of you, and, if you want to know, so was your daughter. Maybe we can collaborate. I've already completed a draft," he said. "I'll e-mail it to you. See what you think."

Mark sent me the following draft:

It all begins with a handgun. Motive? Self-defense. Maybe target shooting. Whether you put it on a credit card, pay cash, or write a check, chances are your explanation to the clerk, if one is required, is perfunctory. It's really pretty simple: "I want to own a handgun."

If self-defense is your motive, do you think about practicing? If that moment comes, can you operate the thing? How does it feel to put a bullet in the chamber? If it's not loaded, you really have to be convincing. What are the odds of convincing someone with another weapon, someone practiced, someone a little amped?

Where will you hide it? From the kids? From that thief who may rob you when you're not at home? A lot of thought has to go into this. It's not a toy anymore. There are a lot of vulnerable houses and apartments in the US. Doors don't lock. Neighbors don't care. There are a lot of cars in America. Cars with registered weapons in the glove compartment. Cars without alarm systems. Cars with alarm systems. And a piece of glass and a mediocre lock between the gun and a person who did not buy it, a person who has but one use for the weapon. It will enable them to take what does not belong to them. It will impress their friends. It will defend their life. But first and foremost, it is for taking.

If someone asked you, "Where does a handgun come from?" you might know a few brand names— Smith and Wesson, Colt. But if someone asked you how did that gun get here where it was never supposed to be, how could you explain it? How did this gun, this taking device, find its way into the hands of a human being who probably never imagined what he or she might do with it and probably never cared? There is no map here. No trail. Just unfortunate moments. People, many people, distanced from the gun, not knowing how close it really is. Three families. One school, yet a district of dozens. A gun takes, and it connects. And this is how it does just that.

A gun, two high school students, and a mother of three children. Random. What does that mean? Wrong place? Wrong time? Bad luck? Or the karmic explanation, that a weapon enables its owner to take, does just that wherever and whenever it wants.

This is an examination of how a handgun found its way into the hands of a high school junior. An examination of a family and school systems that did not detect its presence. And how difficult and frustrating and painful life becomes when society doesn't monitor the sale or possession of handguns effectively enough. Wrongfully, society allows the prevalence of people owning weapons to wantonly murder at an alarming rate.

Mark Shapiro, a kind, caring human being, died in 2011 before he could ever honor his dear friend Susie, who had so valued his friendship.

Chapter
20

When Susie was twelve years old and Eric was eight, we moved from Queens to Great Neck. It was an enlightening experience for them, and they discovered that children of all ages, sizes, and shapes lived on our street. They had experienced just the opposite in our Queens neighborhood. Soon our house became the hangout for all these kids.

Susie formed instant, lifelong friendships with three neighborhood children in particular. Seth Swirsky lived next door, Michael Zeller a few houses away, and Jody Ellant across the street.

As an adult, Seth was distraught over Susie's death. He was now a successful songwriter living in California. Upon hearing the news, he immediately reserved a seat on the red-eye to arrive in New York the following day for her funeral. This was a testimony to the friendship he and Susie enjoyed throughout their teenage years as they lived next door to one another, attended the same high school in Great Neck, and even shared their August birthdays.

It was natural for Seth and Susie to become friends because they had so much in common and so much to talk about. One special connection was a shared appreciation of the latest pop music. Seth was a gifted musician even as a teenager. He considered Susie "one of the guys" because she was lithe and athletic, and their interests in dance and music added to their attachment. Even when attending colleges in different states, with Susie at Skidmore in upstate New York and Seth at Dartmouth in New Hampshire, they remained in contact. Whenever they returned home during school breaks, it was delightful to see their warm response to each other.

They maintained their solid friendship despite differing political views. Prior to elections, a flurry of e-mails between St. Louis and California was like fireworks over the airwaves as each tried to counter the other's opinion. But those differences never altered the warm feelings they had for each other.

Seth made every effort to keep their friendship and her memory alive in an extraordinary way, using his gift of music in honor of Susie's fiftieth birthday. We received a series of e-mails.

"I thought of Susie a lot on her birthday," he wrote. "I mentioned that I had written a song about her. I wanted to do a YouTube®- and Facebook®-type tribute to her as my present to her. I just need some photographs of her at any age. Do you have any you would be willing to FedEx®? The more the better. It's a special song for a special woman."

I e-mailed back, thanking Seth for his gracious offer, and sent him many photographs with a note that read, "I hope I didn't create a monumental job for you."

His response: "Thank you for sending the photos. Fantastic! And please don't feel as if it's any burden; it's the opposite—it's pure joy because it's Susie. She continues to inspire; she always will."

I received the following e-mail a few days later: "These incredible photographs arrived today. I just want you to know they are so great. Just the right amount to choose from and it's so nice 'visiting' with Susie. She brightens up a day with her gorgeous smile and face. Thank you, Lois."

A while later Seth sent another e-mail: "I just wanted you to know that the video is coming out very well. When you make a project like this, with so many photos, you get to 'spend time' with the person in the photos (because you're looking at the photos frequently). It's been such a nice time 'spending time' with Susie. Her gorgeous smile is in my world every day since I started making this. She is a ray of sunshine. I wanted you to know this. It's been like having a week-long visit and it feels really nice."

In still another e-mail, Seth wrote, "I'm so thrilled to be able to get these photos. They'll go so well with the song I've written for Susie. It's a joy to do this because I feel like Susie's there. It's a song that 'feels' like her spirit—very upbeat, happy, freewheeling, enjoyable to be around."

The video was produced after many months of devoted hard work. The title of the song was "Susie Sunshine" and the words were lovingly written. Both captured the essence of Susie. It was not only a tribute to Susie and their friendship but to Seth's consummate artistry as a filmmaker and songwriter.

Seth e-mailed me the words to the song, writing, "This is my gift to you. To Susie. I think about her often and as I've said before, every time she pops into my head, I see her with that classic, wide, happy *smile*. No one had a smile like Susie. *No one!*"

SUSIE SUNSHINE

She was so sweet, like a sister to me
I remember the days we would talk endlessly
listening to records with no thought of the time

Susie Sunshine, Susie Sunshine

on her front lawn
I would sing her my songs
in between cartwheels she'd sing along
even though she didn't know the words half the time

Susie Sunshine, Susie Sunshine

Susie walked with a swingin' step
with a white wristband made of string
vividly, she's still easy to see in her faded jeans with the
hole in the knee

just hangin' round, nothing profound
just her and me and now I believe
every time I see a rainbow, it's a sign

Susie Sunshine, Susie Sunshine

she was so sweet, like a sister to me
I remember the days we would talk endlessly
every time she smiles the world is so fine

Susie Sunshine, Susie Sunshine
Susie Sunshine, Susie Sunshine
Yeah

Seth returned the photos. He included a note that read, "Thank you so much for allowing me to visit with Susie these few months. Her smile—like no other smile—lit up my world. Such a beautiful person. With love, Always Love, Seth."

Several months later the documentary *Beatles Stories*, which Seth wrote, filmed, and produced, was entered into international film festivals. Among them was the Gold Coast Film Festival, which was scheduled to be shown in Great Neck. The film focused on an interview with Norman Smith, the Beatles' first recording engineer, about his experiences working with them, in addition to other personal stories by celebrities who had some connection with the

Fab Four. David and I attended one of the showings because of our love for the Beatles and because it was Seth's artistic achievement. We remembered the connection Susie and Seth had to the Beatles and the encounter Susie had with John Lennon all those years ago in high school. We were deeply touched to see that Seth dedicated his film to Susie. It was a life-affirming experience for all of us. After the performance, Seth, David, and I hugged each other, and I said, "Seth, did you know Susie's story about meeting John Lennon and Yoko Ono when she was in high school? If not, I need to tell you . . ."

Chapter
21

"I think often about how Susie made me smile. How much Rachel, Daniel, and Sarah remind me of Susie and the sorrow I feel whenever I see them. How much I miss her." Like Seth Swirsky, Michael Zeller would often repeat such sentiments about Susie after her death. He said, "She was known for her strong will, determination, yet kindness and a ready smile."

Like so many others, Michael described being immediately attracted by Susie's smile when they met. "She was fun and flirtatious, but a tomboy," he said. "Susie became one of my best friends since seventh grade and, in fact, about my only friend at the time who wasn't a 'real' boy."

On one occasion after Susie's death, Michael reminded me that when he and Susie were in their twenties they became workout partners. "We pumped some iron and went jogging together," he said. Michael hesitated for a moment and then added, "Actually, come to think of it, these were highly competitive, one-on-one, five-mile road races through the streets of Great Neck. I don't recall clearly who won, which means—I guess—that Susie must have won. I tried but was no match for her in fitness. What really mattered, though, is that fitness and friendship were always intertwined."

The friendship was further cemented when Michael met and married Gayle, who is intelligent as well as beautiful. Michael's parents were not only neighbors of ours but also close friends, and the relationship between Michael's family and ours became even more meaningful with Gayle's addition.

One summer, our granddaughter Sarah was visiting us in New York for several days and developed a raging cough and sore throat. Sarah didn't want to miss anything during this visit and didn't think she needed to see a doctor. But after the second day, I became concerned about her condition. Gayle is a pediatrician, so I decided to look to her for medical guidance. It was after 9:00 p.m. when I called Gayle with apologies for bothering her at such a late hour. I told her about Sarah's cough and sore throat.

"Does she have a temperature?" Gayle asked.

"No, but I don't know what to do. She doesn't want me to take her to a doctor, but I don't like to fool around with a cough and sore throat."

"I don't blame you," she said. "I wish she could come to my office so I could check her out, but I'm nowhere near it. This is what I would recommend: take her to Long Island Jewish. They have an all-night children's clinic."

Long Island Jewish Hospital was only ten minutes from our house and would be an easy trip. I thanked Gayle profusely.

"No problem," she said. "I would do anything for Susie and your family."

I called Susie to give her an update about Sarah, her cough, and my conversation with Gayle. Susie listened carefully. "Ma," she said, "Gayle's a good doctor and a really good friend."

"I know, and that's the way she feels about you, too."

Michael and Gayle repeated to me another conversation they

had with Susie shortly before she died. "We talked a lot about Susie's three children and both sets of our remarkable parents. Our families always came first. Fitness and politics were very important, to be sure, but a distant second. Nothing else really mattered." Michael added that Susie had told him how proud she was of her children, that in spite of a contentious divorce, they had matured into beautiful, thoughtful, and caring people. Gayle attributed these qualities to Susie.

Michael told us that he had swapped countless e-mails with the 1978 graduating class at Great Neck South High School to exchange consolations after Susie's death. He said, "We're all mourning the loss of her kindness and indomitable spirit." Then he added, "I think Rachel, Daniel, and Sarah inherited that spirit. Susie Schaffer was someone you could never forget."

Chapter
22

As treasured as Susie's friendships were with Seth, Michael, and Gayle, she shared an equally meaningful friendship with Jody. After Susie's death, Jody wrote the following heart-wrenching reflections on their close relationship, which she shared with me:

"I remember a bright spring day back in 1972. I was twelve years old and a new home was being built on our block, diagonally across the street from my house. The owner of the new home, Lois, called my mom to invite us to a party at the construction site to meet her two children—a girl, Susie, exactly my age, and a boy, Eric, the age of my younger brother. Going over there on that bright spring day, my mind was filled with exciting thoughts. 'What would Susie be like? Would she be fun? Would we be friends?'" And friends they became, instantly.

Jody further describes what happened when she, her mother, and her brother walked across the street for this meeting. "Susie's larger-than-life personality came through within minutes. It felt as if we had struck a special bond. I was struck by the love that emanated from Lois and David toward their children, how they made this incredible, thoughtful effort to make this meet-and-greet for Susie and Eric so that their transition to a new home and a new neighborhood and school would be eased."

Jody shared a quintessential memory about her friendship with Susie during the ice storm in 1973. She wrote:

> Our entire village of Great Neck Estates lost power for five days. I remember a fabulous, fun week filled with exploration and laughter as I spent the entire time with Susie, a vacation into a magical world filled with icicles glittering on all the trees, with the minor inconveniences of no heat, no bathrooms, and no hot water. I recall walking to town on ice-covered streets, slipping, sliding, and laughing all the way. There were no cars, no other people, just Susie and me. When we arrived in town, all of the stores were closed and covered with ice so we turned around and made the long, cold, icy, adventure-filled walk home. When we arrived back at the Schaffers' house, Lois made us some hot chocolate and we tried to warm our then-frozen feet by the fireplace. As I attempted to warm my feet through my three layers of woolen socks, I remember smelling something rather acrid. In looking down at my feet, I saw that my sock had begun to smolder and catch fire. Rather than panicking, Susie and I quickly tore off my first sock through our giggles, marveling at the fact that one's feet could be so cold that it would be impossible to feel the heat of fire. Thirty-eight years later, I still look back at that moment, not with fear, but remembering the love and joie d'vivre that surrounded Susie and all who were so fortunate to be within her inner circle.

Jody volunteered her thoughts regarding Susie's marriage. "I remember being very surprised when I heard Susie was marrying Peter. They seemed so different, he so controlled and she such a free spirit. In retrospect, given my initial reaction to their union, I wasn't surprised that it didn't work out."

Jody's most powerful feelings about their friendship were revealed to me when she said, "It's hard to put into words the essence of a soul, but I would like to at least try. Susie lived each moment of life to the fullest, making for a fun-filled, somewhat rambunctious adolescence for us both."

In one of Jody's notes to me, she wrote:

> In trying to understand the tragedy of what happened to Susie, I have tried to imagine the moments before Susie's death. I can imagine Susie walking into her kitchen, putting down her things, and upon realizing that there were teenagers rifling through her things, not even considering that they might be intent on murder, but rather remembering our own teenage years and her fearless encounters with fire. She might have displayed some of that same bravado that caused us to laugh at my almost-burnt feet. I think she would have said to those boys, 'What the f–k are you doing in my house?' Rather than trying to escape from the situation, if she was physically able to, I imagine that she would have stood her ground, and, remembering the indiscretions of our own youth, would have tried to teach them that whatever was going wrong in their life, they should learn to laugh at it to get through the moment. She would have tried to suggest that they had better things to do with their lives than rummage through

her house for loot. Unfortunate for all of us, these teenagers had acquired a fully-loaded gun and, without a moment's forethought, aimed at Susie and deprived us all forever of her joie de vivre.

Chapter

23

Lynne Marmulstein called us in disbelief just after Susie died. In-between her tears, she said how thrilled she had been after meeting Susie. They discovered each other because they were next-door neighbors in a Chicago apartment complex. They also discovered that they were both newlyweds. Lynne told me that from the very beginning she thought Susie was beautiful, fun to be with, and smart, but she had her doubts about Peter. "I guess I was right," she added.

Their connection deepened with time as they discovered their similar backgrounds and shared stories about their childhood. Lynne said that many times the similarities were so strong they would giggle like little girls.

Their talks included Susie's dream of having her own business, preferably in the field of health and fitness. She added that Susie had a vision of what she could do and how she could do it, given her agility and dance background. She loved sharing her knowledge with others.

"I was so unhappy when Susie moved back to New York, even though I knew it was home for her," Lynne confessed to me.

"I missed the daily contact, our talks, the appreciation of our just being together." Lynne told me Susie had alluded to the fact that she was unhappy in her marriage and the move from her roots had been that much more difficult. Susie also said she was going to do everything in her power to make it work. But her husband, although dedicated to his profession, did not share her cultural values.

Lynne told me they stayed in close contact in spite of distance. "The phone wires were hot," she said. "As we began to have families, our bond grew even stronger. We made a point to schedule visits between Chicago and St. Louis with the children and to share each other's lives. There wasn't anything that we couldn't or didn't share. What we had was so special. We were kindred spirits, sisters of a sort, destined to meet and touch each other's lives in ways that would create a bond as if connected by blood—forever."

My connection to Lynne has grown deeper. It's one of the many means for both of us to keep Susie alive in our minds and our hearts.

Chapter

24

"I can never forget the day I received a call from her father, who simply stated, 'Susie's gone.' At first, I assumed he meant that she had jumped in her car and driven away without telling anyone where she was going. Perhaps she needed some alone time to think; perhaps she hadn't arrived home at a time she was expected."

These were the words Dr. Mary Macedonio tearfully shared with us after Susie's death. She told us, "I remember the sheer devastation that coursed through me when I heard him say she was the victim of a homicide. The news completely wracked my soul. The room around me fell dark and my heart ruptured."

Mary and Susie were longtime friends, and, like Susie, Mary was a passionate, concerned human being. They both held dreams of helping mankind, though by different routes. Susie's passion was to build confidence and strength by means of movement and nutrition. Mary wanted to achieve the same goal by becoming a clinical psychologist. Susie and Mary's friendship was powered by mutual understanding of each other's visions.

Mary shared her impressions of Susie when they first met while living in an apartment complex in Bayside, Queens. "I remember the first time I saw Susie walking on the grounds of our complex. It was a beautiful afternoon, bright and clear, and the sun fell on her curls, illuminating her with light. She reminded me of a poised flower, basking in the glow of the rays. She was truly graceful, moving with fluidity and ease, blotting out the blandness of the uninteresting and ordinary surroundings at the property we shared our lives in."

Mary went on to say, "Over time, I observed Susie's loving tenderness toward her family, the joy her daughter Rachel brought to her heart, and her happiness at being a mother, in addition to her verbalized dreams of someday establishing herself in a teaching role to others."

Like Lynne, Mary was bereft when Susie moved from their apartment complex to another and then, ultimately, to St. Louis. The move to St. Louis was mandated because Peter had received a new job offer. It was the ultimate test of their friendship. But Susie always made time to visit with Mary whenever she flew to New York, and in the meantime they constantly exchanged phone calls and e-mails.

Mary told us that Susie struggled with the decision to relocate for several reasons. Leaving her family was painful, as were her thoughts about the future of her marriage. But Mary went on to say, "There was much anguish, distress, significant concern, and suffering at that time because Susie was moving to another state and out of the realm of her roots and family, all exacerbated by a tenuous marriage. But Susie had the resolve to do whatever it took to keep her family intact and safe."

Susie often told me that she and Mary kept in touch in spite of the distance and their busy schedules. It was quality time for both of them.

Mary went on to say, "I was so proud to see how Susie blossomed as I knew she would, overcoming the personal pain of her divorce and bringing immense joy to so many others by teaching and bestowing her gracefulness upon them."

Then Mary told us what we already knew about Susie and Alvin. Susie consistently referred to him as "the absolute love of my life."

Mary said, "Susie was the sister I never had. She was the epitome of love, joy, and hope, which entwined to form a major part of her spirit. I was always and in all ways graced and honored by my relationship with her."

Mary is a link to the past, with thoughts of happier times we all spent together and the memory of a beautiful friendship.

Chapter
25

The emotions experienced after the loss of a loved one are cogently expressed in Nancy Cobb's book *In Lieu of Flowers*, in which she comments, "Now that I am a mother, I cannot conceive of losing a child to death." She is correct; it is inconceivable. The loss of a child breaks the link to the past, present, and future and is especially devastating under violent circumstances. No one can possibly imagine the unspeakable terror Susie faced during the last crucial moments of her life.

Nancy Cobb continues: "We all expect to experience a parent's death one day, but never a child's. It is as unnatural as it is unimaginable."

Famed author and professor Roger Rosenblatt expresses his grief in his book *Making Toast*, written after the sudden death of his daughter Amy. Although her death was not the result of violence, it was nevertheless untimely. Amy was a successful thirty-eight-year-old pediatrician. His child. Professor Rosenblatt writes: "I cursed God. In a way, believing in God made Amy's death more, not less comprehensible, since the God I believe in is not beneficent. He doesn't care. A friend was visiting Jerusalem when he got the news about Amy. He kicked the Wailing Wall and said, 'Fuck you, God!' My sentiments exactly."

Mary Rondeau Westra's twenty-four-year-old son Peter died because of a brutal beating from a bouncer at an Atlantic City nightclub. In her book *After the Murder of My Son*, she describes her feelings upon hearing of his death: "I felt helpless, adrift, a tsunami barreling over me, tossing me, threatening to drown me."

Ellen Zelda Kessner expressed her grief and initial involuntary reaction after learning of her daughter's death by gunfire. Mrs. Kessner writes: "Sheryl, my firstborn child, is dead. I curl up on the hall staircase in the fetal position wanting to stay there forever; there is no place on earth for me now."

After learning of Susie's death, a friend of mine who is a clinical psychologist vividly expressed her empathy in this metaphor: "There are swamps in life that we can walk around. Others we must slog through. This one you must slog through."

The loss of a child is like a scar that will never disappear. This image touched a nerve when a small basal cell carcinoma was discovered on my face. I had a consultation with a surgeon about its required removal. "You will have a small scar," said the surgeon. "I'll try to make it as small as possible. Nevertheless, you will have a scar. It should disappear in time." After listening to what the kind surgeon was telling me, all I could think of was the scar that remains after our daughter's death. The abysmal emotions we feel can never be small and will not disappear. Time is not a healer in this case. One can only try to cover that scar in a positive manner.

Dr. Dorothy Greenbaum, a pediatrician, mother, mohel (ritual circumcisor), and author, tenderly portrays her journey to becoming a doctor in her moving book *Lovestrong*. One of the reasons she chose this path was her need to act positively, remembering the death of her four-year-old twin brother. During her pediatric rotation as a medical student prior to her internship, Dr. Greenbaum was assigned to a case involving a three-year-old boy with a terminal brain tumor. Empathetically, with her twin brother always in mind, Dr. Greenbaum related to this heart-wrenching experience. The chief of the pediatric department was her warm, supportive advisor during this rotation, and as part of her medical training, Dr. Greenbaum accompanied the kindly advisor to deliver the much-dreaded news to the boy's parents.

Dr. Greenbaum wrote: "I slipped away and walked quickly to the bathroom. I cried in the privacy of a locked stall. There's no way I can go through this again, I thought, no way." Thoughts of becoming a pediatrician became increasingly difficult to handle because, as she confessed, "I can't remain cool and composed while a child is dying." The older, wise doctor understood the infinite sadness that Dr. Greenbaum felt and counseled his student, "Dorothy—every time a child dies, a piece of me dies. No one ever learns to accept the death of a child."

The death of a child to an incurable disease is sad enough. A small consolation is that feelings can be shared before death. However, this is not the case when the death comes without warning, when it is the result of violent, senseless brutality. In one split instant and without warning, our daughter met her tragic demise, as did Christina Taylor Green in Tucson, Arizona, on January 8, 2011.

Dallas Green, described as the "steely" former manager of the Mets, Yankees, and Philadelphia Phillies, was interviewed after the death of his granddaughter, Christina, by journalist Ken Davidoff in his *Newsday* article on February 17, 2011. The husky six-foot-five Dallas Green said, as he tried to stifle his tears, "You know, I'm supposed to be a tough sucker. I'm not really tough when it comes to this."

The monstrous brutality on December 14, 2012, at Sandy Hook Elementary School in Newtown, Connecticut, caused untold devastation among the parents of the murdered children.

In his touching play *Rabbit Hole*, now also a film, David Lindsay-Abaire addresses the aftermath that the parents in his play feel after the shattering death of their four-year-old son, who was hit by a car. Unlike Susie's death, this was not due to gun violence. Nevertheless, like Susie's, it was sudden, violent, and senseless. *Rabbit Hole* depicts the parents and other family members whose lives are inalterably changed forever. It is an erosion that only families like ours, the Rosenblatts, Kessners, Greens, Westras, and the parents in *Rabbit Hole* can relate to.

The loss of a child is unfathomable to begin with, particularly under senseless, violent circumstances. It takes all the strength in a parent's gut to maintain any equilibrium after the initial shock. Devastating as the tragedy is, I believe that one must ultimately focus on the living, which to me means concentrating on the physical and emotional welfare of my husband David, my son Eric, his family, Susie's children, and Alvin, in addition to my own well-being.

Chapter

26

A deep, unsettling sense of despair and gloom pervaded Lois and Ben's home as we entered after arriving from New York. It was the day following Susie's death. Each room was densely populated with people of all sizes, shapes, and ages. Ordinarily this would have produced an ear-splitting din, but it was eerily quiet and somber. The silence was so loud it was deafening.

Rachel quickly spotted her brother and sister. They ran to each other, sank to the floor, and sat cross-legged, in tears, with their heads close and their arms wrapped around each other's shoulders. Alvin saw this scene, dropped to the floor, and put his arms around the three of them.

Lois and Ben's house was a safe haven for all of us. Countless people appeared all day and for the several days we remained in St. Louis. There were our grandchildren's friends, Susie's friends, her colleagues, and the family and friends of Lois, Ben, and Alvin.

In a quiet moment, Alvin poured his heart out to me. "Never did I think anything like this could happen to me. Did you?"

"No, it's unbelievable."

"I would always feel sympathetic if I heard of a violent tragedy. It was always the other guy, not me."

"I know what you mean."

"Now I'm the other guy," he said.

Tears welled up in Alvin's eyes, and I couldn't help but cry too. "Our lives have been changed forever."

"Yes," he continued, bereft. "Unbelievable, senseless loss."

Alvin took out his handkerchief, blew his nose, and wiped his uncontrollable tears. The words just spilled out. "I keep telling myself that tragedies like this don't happen to me, not to my loved ones or anyone I know. After sixty years on this earth, I mistakenly thought I had immunity . . . and would've bet I would be struck by lightning or win a national lottery of a billion dollars before this unspeakable, heinous, unimaginable, unthinkable, senseless murder made me the other guy . . ."

We looked at each other, unable to speak for a moment.

Breaking the silence, I said, "It's comforting for all of us to be together. I bless you for all the love you have shown Susie's children."

"They're great kids. It's wonderful they have been so much a part of my life."

"So now what do we do?"

"Be there for one another."

"That's right."

At that moment, we hugged each other.

In times like this, people want to do something—anything— and so they show up in droves with enormous platters of food to maintain the mourners' physical strength and try to lessen the pain. The sense of camaraderie was so much appreciated. We received countless phone calls and letters from people Susie had formed lasting relationships with. Merchants, coworkers, her children's teachers, and neighbors whose lives she had impacted in varying ways all made it a point to tell us stories of how she had affected them. We knew she had a highly respected reputation, but until then did not really know its extent.

Chapter
27

Our tragedy was news. It was broadcast all over the media, including the St. Louis television channels, radio stations, and newspapers. The two seventeen-year-olds, Kenneth Shepard and Lorenzo Wilson, the trigger-happy shooter, were caught together within twenty-four hours. They confessed. They were easily traced because Shepard was wearing an electronic bracelet due to prior juvenile crimes. The only solace we felt stemmed from their quick apprehension.

Gun violence was anathema to me and Susie. I recalled how she didn't even permit Daniel to play with a water gun. Ironically, I had joined the gun control organization New Yorkers Against Gun Violence in October 2008 after hearing my local assemblywoman, Michelle Schimel, speak passionately about the passage of the Microstamping Bill, first in the assembly and then in the senate. She had coauthored this bill with New York senator Eric Schneiderman, who has since become New York state attorney general. Two months later, Susie was murdered.

Wilson's confession illustrated his evil nature. Even as he confessed to the police that he had been out to shoot someone, he also said he told Shepard to take the gun "because I want *you* to know how it feels to shoot someone." How much this magnified the sharp contrast between an individual like our daughter, whose only purpose was to help humanity, and one who was out to destroy it!

In spite of the devastation we were all feeling, my focus was to do whatever was necessary for all of us. I needed to put into action whatever it took to deal with our catastrophic loss. First we had to decide where our daughter was to be buried. We decided on New York because she was always a New Yorker at heart, even though she had lived in St. Louis for sixteen years. We made arrangements for her funeral, which was held at our synagogue. The overflow of mourners was astounding. More than five hundred people braved the ice and snow of that cold December day. The outpouring of people was a comfort to us.

In a different tragedy, William Sloan Coffin delivered the eulogy for his son after he was killed in an automobile accident during a raging storm. He said to the many mourners, "Love not only begets love, it transmits strength." I agree with Coffin's sentiments. Showing love and strength is important to me. We clutch tighter those we love in attempts to fill the cavernous void caused by death. That was one of the central points I wanted to emphasize at Susie's funeral and for the three months I spent daily writing notes to everyone who had reached out to us—more than five hundred of them. It was a catharsis.

The other point I emphasized was the connection between choice and action. Is it your choice to sit in a corner and suck your thumb, or will you take action by counteracting personal tragedy in a positive, productive manner?

Roger Rosenblatt, whose moving book I discussed earlier, demonstrated how he and his wife took action after his daughter suddenly died of a rare heart condition while exercising on her treadmill. Although it was not gun violence that took her life, her death was nevertheless sudden and traumatic. They took positive action by choosing to help their grandchildren and son-in-law by living with them.

Joyce Gorycki, the widow of James Gorycki, who was slain in the Long Island Railroad massacre by the same gunman as Congresswoman Carolyn McCarthy's husband, has become a staunch activist for the reduction of gun violence since that fateful day in 1993. She has appeared at countless press conferences and on radio, television, and cable networks. She is also the Long Island chairwoman for New Yorkers Against Gun Violence. Her activism has earned her many honors, including a Women of Distinction award from the Seventh Senate District.

Former nurse Carolyn McCarthy chose to take action by running for Congress with a focus on the issue of gun control after her son and husband were victims of gun violence. Her son is still alive, but her husband was mortally wounded. Congresswoman McCarthy's modus operandi to save lives in the medical field was transferred to her congressional candidacy in response to her personal tragedy. During her tenure as an elected official and in spite of several death threats, she launched major campaigns for gun control.

Lee and Jonathan Ielpi, a father and son, were firefighters for the city of New York. Jonathan perished in the September 11, 2001, attacks on the World Trade Center. Lee formed an organization, the September 11 Families Association, which provides counseling and support to those who were deeply affected by the attacks. Additionally, they provide scholarships in memory of those who perished and work closely with the medical examiner to identify remains of the September 11 victims.

Ellen Zelda Kessner's choice was to take action by becoming a vital force in the organization Parents of Murdered Children. Although her daughter, Sheryl, was not a victim of domestic violence, Mrs. Kessner's platform led to educating the public through speaking engagements on teen dating violence and violent marriages. To this end, she appeared on Oprah Winfrey's talk show, published numerous articles on this topic, wrote a book called *After the Violence*, and coauthored *Saving Beauty from the Beast*.

John Green, the father of nine-year-old Christina Taylor Green, and her grandfather Dallas Green took action by immersing themselves in their livelihoods in baseball after the Tucson massacre. Dallas Green said, "It's helped me because you sink yourself into the work. You don't see a little girl with a hole in her chest as much. So I get through it. John, my son, is going to hurt like the devil for a long time."

In his exquisitely written book, *The Thirteen Petalled Rose*, revered rabbi Adin Steinsaltz attributed action to a higher being in the following deeply thoughtful manner:

> The secret of the positive mitzvot, the commandments to perform certain actions lies, in a manner of speaking, in the activization of the limbs of the body, in certain ways of doing things which are congruous with higher realities and higher relationships in other worlds. In fact, every movement, every gesture, every habitual pattern and every isolated act that man does with his body has an effect in whole systems of essences in other dimensions with and against one another. Clearly, an ordinary person does not know anything of this; at best he is conscious only to a very small degree of the things he does and of their higher significance.

My interpretation of Rabbi Steinsaltz's quote is that we partner with God in an attempt to do virtuous acts. I believe such virtuous acts as those demonstrated by Congresswoman Carolyn McCarthy, Ellen Zelda Kessner, the Rosenblatts, Lee Ielpi, and the Greens were done in the hope of trying to counteract tragedies at the same time as they are an integral component of human nature striving to do good.

The deaths of Anne Frank and Hannah Senesh are symbols of the Holocaust. Martin Luther King Jr. is a symbol of the civil rights movement. Jonathan Ielpi is a symbol of 9/11. Our daughter is a symbol of the significant number of people who are murdered every day by gun violence. Our society's consciousness must be raised in order to take urgent action against these senseless deaths by banning the possession of illegal handguns through new and enforceable legislation.

Deeply entwined in our mourning was the legal process that our family experienced. We did not have to face the frustration of locating the thugs because they were apprehended within twenty-four hours. Nevertheless, we learned that we might have to be confronted with not one but two trials because there were two criminals, and the law states that they must be tried individually.

Chapter

28

"Life changes in the instant—the ordinary instant," wrote Joan Didion in her supremely articulated book *The Year of Magical Thinking*, written after experiencing the sudden loss of her husband and daughter in one year.

The death of the four-year-old in *Rabbit Hole* occurred in an "ordinary instant," or during a normal day in that family's daily life. It was an ordinary instant when Mary Rondeau Westra's twenty-four-year-old son Peter was kicked to death by a bouncer on a sidewalk outside a nightclub in Atlantic City, where he had gone to attend a bachelor party. An honor student at Middlebury College, he was a successful investment banker at Deutsche Bank when he succumbed to his untimely and brutal death.

In his 1984 heart-wrenching article in *Vanity Fair*, entitled "A Father's Account of the Trial of His Daughter's Killer," the late, renowned author and investigative journalist Dominick Dunne wrote about his daughter Dominique, who was strangled to death by her psychopathic boyfriend John Sweeney. Although it was not gun violence, it was nevertheless a brutal, senseless act that occurred in an ordinary instant. The sudden death of Ginny and

Roger Rosenblatt's daughter also took place in an ordinary instant. Sheryl Maude Kessner, who was mercilessly murdered by her husband's associate, died in an ordinary instant. The same must be said of the deaths at Sandy Hook Elementary School in Newtown, Connecticut. The mass murders in Tucson, Arizona, specifically the deaths of Judge John Roll and Christina Taylor Green, also occurred in an ordinary instant.

"She embodied what's good about kids, what's good about growing up in the United States"—these words were expressed by Christina's grandfather, Dallas Green. Young Christina had an interest in politics and wanted to be at an event with Senator Gabrielle Giffords. She was "in the wrong place at the wrong time," added Green. And September 11, 2001, was an "ordinary" day, and in an ordinary instant Jonathan Ielpi, along with thousands of others, was murdered.

Susie's death occurred in that ordinary instant. So, too, were David's life and mine changed in an ordinary instant.

I have always considered myself fortunate to have a successful marriage. David and I have been friends since we were sixteen years old. We married at twenty-one and now honor our more than fifty-year marriage. We have experienced other times of sadness in our lives, such as when David's mother died from breast cancer six months before we were married, when she was only fifty-four. His father died at sixty-two and my father at sixty-four. But we were blessed with having my mother alive until age ninety-eight, and, best of all, her thought processes functioned well until the day she died. The expression "she had all her marbles," including a wonderful sense of humor, couldn't have been more suitable. These deaths were sad but expected losses. However, the death of a child has a far greater impact, especially when exacerbated by the unthinkable brutality that caused our daughter's life to be so violently extinguished.

From the very outset of this tragedy, David and I focused on two things: survival and action. The survival of our loving relationship is vital in spite of the devastation we feel and how deeply this tragedy has affected us.

Survival included gathering all the strength we could to bolster and maintain the emotional and physical equilibrium of our grandchildren, in addition to strengthening our relationship with each other. We have heard of some couples who cannot cope with such devastation and are weakened rather than strengthened. Such couples often part as a result.

Our consultations with a grief counselor were meaningful and cut to the core of our innermost feelings. Our counselor listened with her trained, understanding ear to the impact Susie had on our lives, not only as her parents but also as lasting friends as she matured. She also impressed upon us that we should enjoy life and not feel guilty about having fun and enjoying pleasurable experiences.

David and I never spoke of how we would preserve our loving relationship. Rather, we demonstrated it by continuing the normal things we did before our daughter's death. The absence of the need for words was beautifully demonstrated on our last trip to Israel, taken in November 2011 after our daughter's death.

We drove to Jerusalem and visited the Western Wall. Those who have been there know that men and women are only allowed to enter from opposite sides. David and I separated and walked to each of our permitted sides. I felt the tears well up as I got closer to the site. I saw multitudes of women of all ages who were sitting or standing, praying, or crying, as I was uncontrollably doing, too. I sat for a few moments in one of the provided chairs, appreciating the significance of this site, and then I wrote a note to Susie to insert in one of the crevices. Briefly, I stated that I knew she had always wanted to return to Israel as an adult, and, unlike Professor Rosenblatt's friend who cursed God for not being there, I believed her spirit was there to help me push on. Then I returned to David. Without a word, we hugged each other and cried.

Dance is unspoken art. No one has expressed the emotions of sorrow through wordless movement better than Martha Graham. In Graham's short, nuanced work "Lamentation," which was choreographed in 1930, the viewer is immediately struck by how Graham was able to express complete sorrow through movement. It is not meant as a study of one person's sadness; it is the embodiment of sadness itself. Graham said "lamentation is tragedy that obsesses the body." She spoke about an incident that occurred after she had performed the work, when a woman who had obviously been crying spoke to her. "You'll never know what you've done for me," she said. The woman related the story of her nine-year-old son, who had been hit by a truck while she watched, unable to save him. The devastation she felt was overwhelming, but she had been unable to cry. The dance work awakened those necessary and therapeutic emotions. Graham responded by saying that "grief is honorable and universal," and the woman needed to cry for her son. Graham said, "There is always one person to whom you speak in the audience." This is another example of how our lives can change in an "ordinary instant," and it expresses the desolation felt after the loss of a child. Graham's work demonstrates how artistry can help another person and points toward both the need to acknowledge tragedy and the need to cry.

One must cry. But then one must focus on action. Our action was manifested in various ways. We concentrated even more intently on the emotional well-being of our grandchildren, for while David and I have each other, we know how deeply our grandchildren feel the effects of their mother's death. We are fortunate to connect with Alvin, and Lois and her family, whose presence in our lives as extended family and friends has become so meaningful. Like Carolyn McCarthy, we have also become involved in efforts to ban the possession of illegal handguns. We emphasize our pride in having a thoughtful, loving son, along with his wife and family. David and I maintain our friendship, not only as husband and wife but as people who have experienced and continue to experience a valued history together.

Feelings of devastation can be acknowledged in an ordinary instant, but life-affirming action must also be taken to counteract losses. One form of action is to say the "Kaddish" prayer. It is an ancient Jewish tradition and an act of loving kindness meant to enable the departed soul to ascend to higher realms. It is also an affirmation of life. Nowhere in the prayer is death mentioned.

We wholeheartedly say "Kaddish," not only so that our daughter may ascend to a higher realm, if there is one, but because it affirms her life and maybe our lives as well.

Chapter

29

Six weeks after Susie's death, we received a phone call in New York from Michael Uthoff, the artistic and executive director of Dance St. Louis, a non-profit organization. Michael told us that Dance St. Louis was going to honor Susie at a performance given by the noted dance company Pilobolus. He thought this would be a perfect venue for a tribute to her talent and passion for movement and the impact she had on many people as a fitness, Pilates, and Gyrotonic instructor.

Ruthe Ponturo, who is actively involved with Dance St. Louis, had introduced Susie to the company. Michael had also ultimately become a student of Susie's.

As parents, we appreciate our children's accomplishments just because they're our flesh and blood, but it's hard to appreciate them fully until we see how others regard our child. At the performance, we were deeply touched by the sentiments expressed by all those who were present and knew Susie on either a professional or personal level. People emphasized how much they admired her commitment to her work and her efforts to be the best possible teacher and communicator. They spoke about her exuberance and love of life as well as dance. It was a just and fitting tribute to Susie.

I vividly recall joyful instances associated with dance that we shared. Susie and I used to drive into Manhattan to take classes at the Martha Graham School of Contemporary Dance. Sometimes we were in different classes, but occasionally we took a class together during her teenage years before she went away to college. This was especially meaningful to me, because like any other teenager she could be moody, difficult, and bossy. However, it was a different story whenever we went to class. Here, she knew she had to behave, because she was among people she considered role models in their profession. Her behavior was impeccable. She made every effort to improve her technique instead of acting like a capricious teenager.

These classes were known as "the Graham School." When you entered its doors, it felt like you were walking on hallowed ground. Although warmth pervaded the halls and friendships developed, it was "serious stuff," populated by people who were passionate about this world-renowned school and company. Members of the company taught the classes and they were always well attended. I remember taking a class with Susie taught by Pearl Lang, the acclaimed dancer-choreographer and one of our favorite instructors. After taking a class together, we talked on our drive home about the various exercises and movement combinations. It was extraordinary to share this experience as mother and daughter.

The two of us had an unspoken rule. We made sure we positioned ourselves on opposite sides of the room during class to demonstrate, especially to ourselves, that we were independent individuals. In this crowded class, Susie placed herself in the front row and I found a place in the last row for the floor exercises.

Pearl Lang stopped the class for a moment to comment on an exercise the students were doing; then she asked a question. We all looked at each other. There was complete silence. No one knew the answer to her question except me. After what seemed like an interminable silence, I answered Pearl's question.

"That's correct," Pearl said as she gestured in appreciation with a fist-bump in the air. Her eyes surveyed the room. "But who said that?"

A distinctive voice piped up from the front row, "That was my mom." A burst of laughter filled the room as Susie turned around to blow me a kiss.

Another memorable instance involving dance happened when Rachel was three. Our family was invited to a reception where a music trio had been hired to play, and Rachel could not contain herself. She ran out onto the floor, dancing in time to the music. Susie and I looked at one another and without hesitation joined her. We jubilantly danced together, all three holding hands.

Another time, I had purchased tickets to a dance concert for our family when Susie was coming to New York for a long weekend. Daniel balked when he learned what we had planned. We were all in the kitchen having breakfast. "You want me to go to a dance concert? You've got to be kidding," he bellowed. First, Rachel tried to convince him that he would like it, but to no avail. Then Susie spoke. "Daniel," she said, "would I ever steer you wrong?"

Daniel sat with his arms folded against his chest, lower lip jutting out. "I'm not going!"

Susie listened calmly. She understood why a nine-year-old boy would be reluctant to attend a dance performance. "That's for sissies!" Daniel shouted.

Still, in her gentle way, Susie was determined to persuade Daniel to go. "Daniel, you like sports. Think of this as basketball players. You'll be amazed at how high the men in the company can run and jump. The dancers are so well trained that you think they're athletes. Also, there's music. You like music—and besides, we can all be together as a family and have a nice dinner in a restaurant afterward."

But Daniel continued to sit silently with his arms crossed in front of his chest.

Susie looked at David. "Dad, please help me. I know he would enjoy it if he would just go."

David scratched his head, wondering what to say. "Daniel, you've never been to a dance concert. What your mother says is correct. It's very exciting to watch and a chance to do something fun together while you're visiting. I love to go, and Grandma and I go to as many concerts as we can."

Daniel looked intently at his grandfather because David was a role model for him in many ways and, most of all, as a nine-year-old he respected David's athleticism.

"I'll tell you what. Give it a try. The worst thing that will happen is that you won't like it and we all promise that we won't force you to go again. I know I speak for your mother as well."

Daniel's arms uncrossed and his lip returned to its normal position. "OK," he mumbled, "but just this time."

The bottom line is that Daniel was mesmerized by the dancers. "Ma," he volunteered after exiting the theater, "you were right. It was great. I can't wait to go again, but never tell the guys that I went. I'll never hear the end of it."

"Daniel, you know I'll never snitch, but they might have the same reaction if they're lucky enough to go. However, for the moment, this is our secret."

I cannot go to a dance concert without thinking of Susie, and of how much we both appreciated this art form and the fact that we were able to share the experience together. I still attend as many dance concerts as possible. However, when the lights go down, my tears well up.

There are so many fond memories of parties, weddings, Bar Mitzvahs, and Bat Mitzvahs. I remember the delight I always felt when we joined together for the traditional, joyful hora.

After Susie died, it took several tries before I could dance while attending a reception with music accompaniment because Susie and I derived so much joy from the blending of the occasion, music, and dancing. It was particularly difficult when the music broke out for all the guests to join in the hora. Finally, I took the plunge at a cousin's wedding. There I was, dancing to celebrate the occasion and honor Susie but fighting back my tears. It felt like the scene at the end of the film *Zorba the Greek* when Zorba dances on the beach following the death of the woman he loved. I think about the famous Rabbi Nachman of Bratslav who also experienced the death of his child. It has been written that Rabbi Nachman coped with tragedy by dancing. Who knows? Maybe dancing is the best way to express deep-rooted sadness.

At the tribute concert, Susie's former rabbi rushed up to me during the intermission. Our conversation was extremely poignant. He said he always marveled at Susie's energy, the way she seemed to juggle her many roles so easily and still focus on her Jewish identity. The rabbi said she was always on time for her children's Hebrew education, running off to teach one of her classes and still having a sandwich prepared to hand her children in case they got hungry. The rabbi's description confirmed what others who connected with Susie had repeatedly said. He concluded by saying, "Her kindness and spirit was a force you could never forget once you met her."

After the performance, I spoke to Michael Uthoff to convey how much we had all loved his tribute to Susie. I then told him I was planning to write a book, both as an illustration of her life and to highlight the need for gun control. I asked for any insight he could give into their relationship, and he sent me the following letter:

I hope that what I can contribute to your book and to the closure of such a painful experience is helpful.

In today's everyday life, all you have to do is open the newspaper and the shocking reality is that the first couple of pages deal only with the senseless murder and death of innocent people. Much too often, we simply shake our heads, aghast.

Over a year ago, a friend, a new friend, was gunned down by two youths on a joy ride. How do you come to grips with anything as stupid as that? Having seen Susan's zest for life, and her passion for helping her fellow man, and her love for dance, I could not help but bond with her.

When reality came crashing in, I felt that the only thing I could do was to honor her life by dedicating one of our performance series to her and her family. It was not only to raise awareness of her life but also the need for gun control.

We remember her for her openness and buoyancy and I know that her spirit is floating all around us.

Ruthe Ponturo and I have become close friends, not only because of our mutual connection to Susie but also for our shared interests in theater, music, art, dance, and fitness, which were all Susie's passions. Once, when Ruthe and I were talking about the tribute to Susie, we relived that meaningful evening and how much Susie would have loved the performance. Ruthe expressed how much she and Susie had cared for one another. Then she said, "Lois, I have lost young friends from incurable illnesses or tragic accidents. Sad or sudden as they were, they were beyond our control. But I cannot and will not ever get over the willfulness of those criminals. I miss Susie terribly, but I can't imagine how you and David function."

Chapter

30

May 2009 was approximately five months after Susie's death. Daniel was graduating from high school, and David, Rachel, Eric, and I were going to fly to St. Louis to attend the ceremonies. I know that each of us was filled with apprehension. It was the first time after Susie's death that we traveled to St. Louis, other than the time we went to attend the concert in her honor. It was alien even to think about being in St. Louis without Susie there, especially for such a milestone event such as Daniel's graduation. I kept telling myself Susie's spirit would prevail. This was my rationale, but it was not Susie in the flesh. I imagined her beaming face were she alive to experience it and know that her son, like Rachel before him, had achieved this goal. I imagined her laughing and hugging everyone in sight, confirming this was an event to be proud of. I imagined her as the "quintessential Jewish mother," bringing healthy snacks for everyone should they get hungry during the ceremonies and before our celebration at a favorite restaurant. But that wasn't the reality. Susie's presence was missing. It was just us, and it was up to each of us—Daniel's grandparents, sisters, uncle Eric, and Alvin— to attempt to fill the missing link. This event was supposed to be one of unadulterated joy. Instead, it carried with it a mixture of bittersweet emotions.

We all made a valiant effort outwardly to relax and smile, acknowledging the importance of Daniel's high school graduation. But we all knew what each of us was thinking and feeling. Tears welled up in my eyes as I also saw David, Eric, and Alvin fighting back their own tears. Many of Susie's friends and parents of other graduates greeted David and me with warm hugs. It was clear they related to our emotional upheaval; they said nothing, but their demeanor was sharply understood.

The ceremony took place in the high school gym to accommodate all of the graduates' families and friends. The sounds of conversation, laughter, congratulations, hugs, and kisses seemed to only magnify what our family was missing. I had always promised myself that I would not make a hopeless situation worse for others or myself though, and I had to give credence to this milestone for the sake of us all. This included Susie's memory. It may have been my imagination, but our family seemed to form more of an attachment that night, one holding us together like invisible glue.

When the graduation ceremony concluded, we met for dinner at one of Susie's favorite restaurants. We made a toast to our time together and a special toast to Susie because her energy and spirit were deeply felt.

David, Eric, and I returned home knowing the next time we would travel to St. Louis would be to attend one of the killer's trials.

Chapter
31

Eighteen months had elapsed since Susie's murder. Lorenzo Wilson, the shooter, and Kenneth Shepard, the other thug, had been in jail since that fateful day. John Quarenghi, the prosecuting attorney, and Lisa Jones, the victims' coordinator, remained in constant communication with our family. Alvin, David, and Eric maintained a personal connection, but it was Eric who made this his all-consuming mission.

We received a phone call in mid-June 2010 from the prosecuting attorney informing us that Shepard's attorney had advised him to plead guilty. This is known as a blind plea. The perpetrator pleads guilty but leaves the sentence to the hoped-for leniency of the judge. The defense attorney pleaded for what was to us a shockingly light ten-year sentence. The prosecuting attorney then demanded a far more fitting thirty-year term. Ultimately, the judge would make the final decision on sentencing after hearing the defense's and prosecuting attorneys' arguments.

The only positive thing for us was that Daniel and Rachel would not have to be put through the painful experience of having to testify as witnesses. Although they were not physically present during the shooting, Rachel was on the phone with her mother during the burglary and Daniel was the first to find her. If a trial were to take place, both would have been considered witnesses.

Needless to say, we all hoped Shepard would get the maximum sentence allowed by law, but that was not to be. The prosecutors advised us to write impact statements for the judge's sentencing consideration. The judge was inundated with these statements, not only from us as Susie's family but from many friends who expressed how they felt about this immeasurable loss to them as well as society.

Eric, David, and I made the gut-wrenching trip from New York to St. Louis to meet with Alvin, Rachel, Sarah, and Daniel for the sentencing, which was scheduled for late June. Although it was sunny and hot, we felt chilled as we gathered at the courthouse to meet the prosecutors for the sentencing. We all felt uneasy knowing we were going to come face to face with this criminal. In her usual supportive manner, Alvin's sister Lois, along with her daughter Elizabeth, joined us.

Lisa Jones met us before we entered the courtroom. Eric, David, and Alvin had held many conversations with her during the eighteen months after Susie's murder. They had described Lisa as smart and kind. Her deep blue eyes, exuding comfort, understanding, and warmth, seemed to penetrate into our souls. Lisa guided us into the courtroom and explained the process about to take place.

We were sitting in the courtroom when a door suddenly opened and this thug emerged from the doorway, handcuffed, shackled, and surrounded by security guards. I had to take a deep breath. This was one of my daughter's murderers. He was ushered into a seat by the security guards, the charges were read, and then his attorney pled his case, followed by the prosecuting attorney.

Our family was told that we could make additional verbal statements before the sentencing. Alvin and Eric chose to do so.

Because of the uncontrollable torment he felt, Alvin had asked Lisa to read a portion of his statement.

"We are victims of the most tragic loss—a loved one's traumatic death and haunting, post-traumatic stress. No one can comprehend this devastation until, tragically, they are also victims. Murder is an inescapable evil that spreads like cancer, burns horror into memory and soul, and brings death to hopes and aspirations." He beseeched the judge "to impose the most punitive sentence and maximum time allowed by law for this unspeakable murder in order that true justice prevails."

It was now Eric's turn to speak. He rose from his seat, and then walked to face the presiding judge's chair. At the same time, he positioned himself to look into the criminal's eyes, which were focused ahead into the distance without any visible expression of remorse. Eric was direct and spoke forcefully of the need for justice to punish this criminal, "to sentence him to the maximum amount of prison time you can under the law and sentencing guidelines."

Eric began by saying that the judge had never met Susie, and trying to relate the essence of a person to someone who has never known her is very difficult. He described Susie as a loving sister: "I struggle to find the words that can capture how lucky a guy I was to have a big sister who loved me, loved her kids, loved her soul mate Alvin, loved her parents, and loved her nephews and niece (my children). It seems a monumental task that words alone could never capture. Susie was a vibrant, beautiful, and passionate person. She loved life and you could feel her vibrancy when she walked into a room. Her presence was a gift that so many of us lost so violently on December 16, 2008. Unfortunately, these are just words, and after a few hours or days their sound and meaning will have vanished into the air as quickly as her beautiful life came to a crashing, unjustified, illogical, and senseless end."

Eric described Susie as a loving single mother, meeting the challenges that this role demanded; listed her accomplishments as a fitness instructor; and explained the rigorous schedule she adhered to between her single motherhood and the joyful but time-consuming pressures she experienced after she opened her own business, which was starting to flourish at the time of her death.

Eric concluded his statement: "Your honor, I know you probably read hundreds of these victim impact statements a year for other very heinous crimes committed against equally devastated families. I only hope that this victim impact statement, this heartfelt letter to you—a thinking, breathing, reasoning human being—will help you to understand that the only way to give us some closure is for you to give this perpetrator the maximum amount of prison time you can." Eric broke down crying as Lisa hugged him at the conclusion of his statement.

Chapter
32

Shepard was sentenced to only twenty years of jail time with the possibility of parole after seventeen. To us, it was a travesty for this criminal to be sentenced to so short a prison term for such a heinous crime. His attorney gave the rationale that Shepherd was only out for robbery, not for a homicide, had fled the house before the shots were fired, and did not fire a gun. The prosecuting attorney then demanded a far more fitting thirty-year term.

Logic tells me that it doesn't matter whether the sentence is twenty or a hundred years. Nothing is going to bring our daughter back. My family and I feel the void every day. What matters are the steps we can take against senseless gun violence such as we have experienced.

Unlike the Westra, Dunne, and Kessner families, we did not have to endure the torturous experience of a long trial following their children's brutal murders. Ultimately, Peter Westra's murderer was only sentenced to seven years of imprisonment and was paroled after a short time. Similarly, the Kessner family suffered the agony of a lengthy trial. Their daughter's murderer was only sentenced to thirty-six and a half years of imprisonment. Though he was denied parole twice, that was small consolation. Also unjustly, John Sweeney, Dominique Dunne's murderer, only received six and a half years of imprisonment due to his inequitably slanted legal representation.

Dominick Dunne stated in his article: "We thought of revenge, the boys and I [his sons], but it was just a thought, no more than that, momentarily comforting. We believe in God and in ultimate justice, and the time came to let go of our obsession with the murder and proceed with life."

I think this statement further confirms our belief that the only logical thing to do is to move on, or more to the point, "push on." Lisa and John emphasized this advice as well. Nothing will bring Peter Westra, Dominique Dunne, Sheryl Kessner, or Susie Schaffer back to life, no matter what sentence the murderers receive. We needed to concentrate on carrying on with our lives, attempting to achieve some normalcy for ourselves and our grandchildren, and prepare for a second trial.

Chapter

33

The influence one individual has on the lives of others is not often appreciated—rather, it is taken for granted. Sometimes it is only truly understood upon that person's death. This was made apparent by the impact Susie's absence had on the lives of her children, particularly Rachel and Sarah. Both girls no longer had a kind and loving mother, nor did they have a father in the true sense of the word. The girls looked to Peter for support even though their relationship was strained since their parents' divorce. At first, it seemed he was going to be there for them; however, that hope was short-lived.

Rachel recalled her father doting on her before the divorce, but everything drastically changed afterward. She wondered whether her father loved her. Sarah had never received care or love from her father, so both girls were stunned when he and his wife Dee volunteered to care for them. Dee, who quit her job as a nurse, turned out to be a compassionate person who tried her best to make their lives as normal as possible.

In spite of an acrimonious divorce, Susie had made sure her children were cared for and loved. It was Alvin who quickly filled the male role. Even though he was not their father, he treated the girls like his own flesh and blood. Daniel's situation was different as far as his father was concerned, for he did not feel the same neglect as the girls. In Peter's mind, boys were easier to relate to, and the girls were replicas of Susie who continually angered him. It must be stated that this is only conjecture, though it's a possible truth. However, I have heard Peter say on occasion, "I just don't understand women." An analyst might have a field day with this father. He may even have been a basic misogynist.

As mentioned earlier, many instances evidenced his anger and negative treatment of Rachel. She felt confusion when he adored her for the first five years of her life, then changed abruptly in his attitude toward her. Then there was the transfer from Boulder to college in New York, the misunderstanding that ensued over the credits she had earned, and his refusal to subsidize the cost for these extra credits she needed to graduate. We were grateful that he paid for the costs of the paralegal program when Rachel dropped out of school.

Like her mother, Rachel is nurturing as well as compassionate. She moved back to St. Louis to be with her sister and brother after Susie died. Although Rachel was glad to be with them, the return to St. Louis raised too many painful feelings for her.

She made a valiant attempt to return to school, but her mother's death had hit her too severely, and she was unable to focus on schoolwork. Her heart and mind were filled with inexorable sadness. Her situation was like a boil that festers and then suddenly erupts, spreading the infection. For a while, her father miraculously understood. He realized that she had experienced an unthinkable loss. After living in St. Louis for a little more than a year, Rachel told her sister and brother that for her own mental health she needed to return to New York.

David and I are proud and relieved to see that she is functioning very well as a paralegal and has made new friends in and out of the law firm. She moved in with us for sixteen months but wisely knew that she needed to be independent and eventually moved into her own apartment.

Sarah got several tattoos. We all tried to dissuade her from doing this, Rachel most of all. We realize that tattoos are not regarded with the same negative connotations today as they were years ago. Nevertheless, none of us approved. Susie never would have approved, especially in light of the fact that she regretted getting one at Sarah's age. We surmised that Sarah did it because the tattoos remind her of Susie, or because she wanted to feel physical pain on the outside like she was feeling inside. It was a cry for help, and her father was not there for her.

Dee made the house she lived in with Peter as comfortable as possible for the children. Peter also tried for a while. He even paid for an apartment for Rachel, finally realizing it was in her best interest to live by herself at twenty-four years of age. It also appeared that Peter and Sarah were initiating a relationship they had never shared before. We then learned that Peter was divorcing Dee because he had become involved in a relationship with another woman. This woman had a family of her own and was in the process of getting a divorce.

That was the last straw for Sarah. Like Susie, she has the capacity to express herself to her father in no uncertain terms. "You had your chance with me and blew it. You are one f-----g idiot."

Julie continually tried to help Sarah in every way she could. "This was the promise Susie and I had made to each other so many years before, should anything happen to either one of us," Julie said, crying during one of our many telephone conversations. "I want to be there for Sarah, not as her mother. She had a mother and a wonderful one. But she won't let me."

"Julie, I understand how you feel. But I think Sarah has distanced herself from you and your family because you're the reminder of what she had and no longer has."

Daniel has buried himself in schoolwork and his fraternity at college and has maintained superior grades. He is not one to articulate his feelings, but his silence is unbearably loud.

Rachel's withdrawal from school, Sarah's tattoos and distancing herself from people like Julie and her family, and Daniel's silence all show the jarring reality of their bereavement—how the loss of one person can so deeply impact the lives of those left behind.

We find solace in making our circle tighter with the help and love of our own friends and our adopted St. Louis family: Alvin, his sister Lois, and her husband Ben, their children, Julie and her husband, Don Eisenberg. They are the links that will help us bear the loss we have all suffered.

Chapter
34

It was almost two years since the shooting. Both thugs were in jail, while we tried to carry on with our lives as well as we could.

In early November 2010 we received an e-mail from Lisa with new information she had just gotten from the prosecuting attorney, John Quarenghi, regarding the shooter, Lorenzo Wilson. She stated that the public defender had approached John about a plea for Wilson, saying that her client would take thirty years on a second-degree murder charge plus ten consecutive years for armed criminal action.

We were all hoping for murder in the first degree because the perpetrator had committed a cold-blooded murder. However, as Lisa and John explained in detail to us and we also knew, if he pled to murder one, the only sentence available would be life in prison without probation or parole, ever. He did not intend to plead guilty to murder one, as there was no upside for him. He would be better off taking his chance that a jury would find him guilty of the lesser count of murder two.

Lisa continued, "The only way he'll plead guilty is if our office comes down off murder one and he would plead to murder two.

Right now, John isn't inclined to do that. The defense attorney's offer wasn't enough jail time as far as John is concerned." We all agreed.

There were several other e-mails that circulated among us the following day, in addition to a conference call.

Daniel sent us an e-mail that reflected his clear assessment: "I also think that murder two is out of the question."

We all concurred and rejected this plea because second-degree murder implies parole. With the additional ten years, the perpetrator would be eligible for parole in about thirty-five years because according to the legal system only 85 percent of a sentence is required to be served. This would mean the shooter would be out on the streets again while still relatively young.

Our family and John were in total agreement that while nothing could bring our daughter back, we wanted the shooter to get the maximum amount of prison time, so this plea was sorely inadequate. Lisa's e-mail continued: "As John and I have said all along, going to trial is a risk for both sides. I am fully confident that with the right jury there is a strong possibility of a murder one conviction. But as always, you never know what you're going to get in a jury pool."

How right Lisa was. I couldn't help but think of the horrific outcome for the trials of the criminals who murdered Peter Westra, Dominique Dunne, and Sheryl Kessner. We focused on waiting for the trial that we all feared but felt was our only choice. It was scheduled for early December.

Chapter

35

In mid-November, we received another e-mail from Lisa. The defense attorney had indicated that the defendant would plead guilty to murder two and robbery one and take two consecutive life sentences on both these counts. However, a life sentence on these charges, she said, means *only* thirty years. Alvin, Eric, David, and I were grateful for this development. At least we would not have to go through the horrendous experience of a trial, and more importantly, Rachel and Daniel would be spared having to testify.

Lisa said the perpetrator would plead guilty to the remaining counts of burglary and armed criminal action and those sentences would run concurrently. For both murder two and robbery one, the criminal must serve 85 percent of his sentence. This meant the perpetrator would serve fifty-one to fifty-four years before being eligible for parole. In other words, he would be approximately seventy years of age. "If he lives that long," Lisa added.

Lisa's e-mail continued: "Both John and I feel confident that we understand where each of you are coming from based on our last phone conversation, and we will communicate your thoughts to our boss, Bob McCulloch."

Rachel was adamant about a trial, and a series of e-mails was exchanged among Rachel, Eric, and David. Rachel said, "I don't care how hard or painful a trial would be. It's nothing worse than I've already been through, and if I hear the shooter is convicted of murder one without the possibility of parole, a trial is beyond worth it for me. He will die in jail and never have a chance of getting out. That's what I want and will not be satisfied with anything less. I *despise* the idea of him getting murder two. It makes me ill."

Eric replied, "I understand how you feel completely. He could also get murder one and live as long in jail as he could getting the sentence Lisa talks about. In other words, we go through the heartache of a trial for no better sentence. Either way, no one wins."

In his infinite wisdom, David tried to reason with Rachel as well. "Rachel, think of it this way. It doesn't matter whether it's called murder one or two. As long as you get the maximum amount of years, that's the important thing."

In a subsequent e-mail, Rachel wrote, "Well, at the end of the day, the prosecutor's office makes the final decision. Obviously, we have a difference of opinion regarding the topic, so I guess we'll just have to wait and see if they take the deal or not."

Lisa responded in her usual thoughtful manner: "I realize there is nothing we could do to this individual that would begin to bring justice for your family. He deserves to be convicted of murder one, but there are always risks when we take a case to trial. Bob McCulloch will weigh the facts of the case, the risks, and the opinions that you've shared with us, and he'll make a decision in the next day or two."

In spite of the emotional upheaval I felt, as I read further into Lisa's e-mail I was comforted by her kindness and sensitivity. She sent another e-mail directly to Rachel with copies to David and Eric. "I know you were passionate about our office not agreeing to any kind of plea negotiation and John will share that with Bob. I think both you and Daniel feel very strongly about that. David and Eric, you were also very clear in what you felt would be best for you and your family. I've also had a conversation with Alvin to bring him up to speed with where we were after our conference call. If we decide to make the deal, we would allow the defendant to plead guilty, but defer sentencing until Monday, December 6, so that the family can be present to make any statements to the judge in front of the defendant."

The following day, we received another e-mail from Lisa confirming the plea would take place on November 19 and the sentencing was scheduled for December 6, 2010.

Chapter
36

All of us tried to keep emphasizing how grateful we were that we would not have to face a second trial. However, the idea of coming face to face with Lorenzo Wilson, the cold-blooded shooter and our daughter's killer, would be even worse than facing Kenneth Shepard.

David said he was going to be there to represent the family. I told him, "If you're going, I'm going."

"You don't have to," he said. "I know Alvin will be there and we'll support each other."

"Honey, I will not let you go alone, even though Alvin will be there."

"I was just trying to spare you," David said.

"I know that, but we're in this together."

"OK, I'll make our plane reservations."

Eric called the next day to say he would be going as well.

We received another e-mail from Lisa. She said that victim statements are always accepted and to let her know if any of us wanted to speak. She added that it would not have any bearing on the sentencing because the plea bargain had already been set. However, a statement is encouraged in order to confront the perpetrator and allow for emotional impact. I told Lisa I was going to make a statement but did not want to tell David until the day of the sentencing.

"I love the way you guys protect each other," she said.

"Lisa, he's my husband and my best friend. David even tried to persuade me not to go to the sentencing in order to protect me."

"In any case, your secret is safe with me," she said. "I'll meet you on December 6, 1:15 p.m., outside of the courtroom." Lisa hesitated for a moment, but then said, "I'll be glad to read it aloud for you if you want."

"Thanks, but no. I think it has more impact if it's delivered by the victim's family."

"I totally agree with you," Lisa answered, and hung up.

David and I had a chance to share our feelings on the flight from New York to St. Louis. We confirmed to each other that while the sentencing would never bring closure to this tragedy, it was the key to moving on with our lives and the lives of our son, his family, and our grandchildren. In the course of our conversation, David said, "I wrote a statement."

I couldn't help but smile and replied, "So did I."

Eric, David, Alvin, and I arrived at the courthouse. We waited for Lisa to meet us outside the designated courtroom. Lois; Ben; their daughter, Elizabeth; their son, Scott; his wife, Jenny; and Ben's brother, David, appeared. No words were spoken; they weren't necessary. We sensed the tears being fought back and resorted to long, hard hugs.

Lisa arrived and we followed her into the large, empty courtroom, which was the same room used for Kenneth Shepard's sentencing. We all huddled in one spot, sitting on benches toward the back. As I looked around, I noticed a woman sitting alone on the other side who was looking down at the floor and then eyeing our group.

"Is that Wilson's mother?" I asked Lisa.

"I think so, but I'm not sure because no one has ever appeared during any of his legal proceedings."

"I wonder why he finally pled?"

"We were shocked as well because he would have been at risk. Usually, a kid this age will go for that risk at a trial. However, he knew that his videoed confessions were self-incriminating, and I think he didn't want to put whatever family he has through that process."

"I didn't know he had any feelings. The police chief described him to us as 'pure evil.'"

We all continued to sit, waiting for the sentencing to begin. I kept watching this lone woman far across the aisle, where she still appeared to alternate between hanging her head and eyeing our group. If this was Wilson's mother, what could she be thinking? I know I was thinking that if this was her son, she had to be ashamed because he committed the most tragic crime, one that created monumental pain and suffering for all those who loved Susie. Not only was I thinking about Susie as a mother but also as a victim of illegal handguns and the system that lets them end up in the hands of criminals like Lorenzo Wilson. Silently, I concluded that this lone woman sitting across the aisle must be Wilson's mother.

On a larger scale, I believed this crime violated the most basic principles of humanity, as have the Holocaust, 9/11, racial violence, the Inquisition, the Crusades, and countless other abominations. Martin Luther King Jr. said, "Injustice anywhere is a threat to justice everywhere" (Letter from Birmingham jail, April 16, 1963). Man's inhumanity to man continues.

We gathered in this courtroom to carry out the laws of justice and uphold our consciences within the boundaries of the legal system in St. Louis; we attempted to counteract this horrible crime while upholding the sanctity of a life that was so cruelly cut short.

I recalled the wisdom of Mohandas Gandhi, who said, "There is a higher court of justice and that is the court of conscience. It supersedes all other courts."

My thoughts were suddenly interrupted when a door opened. We all looked at each other. My stomach seemed to jump into my mouth and I felt like I was choking. It was Susie's murderer, who shuffled in, handcuffed and shackled, with two guards on either side of him. It was a surreal sight to behold as the guards ushered him to a seat. The judge walked in and took his appointed seat at the bench as the guards escorted Lorenzo Wilson to face him. I later learned that this was the highly respected St. Louis County circuit judge John Ross.

"We are here on the matter of the state of Missouri versus Lorenzo Wilson. Are you the same Lorenzo Wilson who pled guilty on November 19, 2010?" asked Judge Ross.

Wilson's response was an almost inaudible "Yes."

The judge then addressed the public defender. "Are you presenting your client for sentencing?"

"I am."

The judge then faced Wilson again and said, "Before I pronounce sentence, have you had enough time to discuss your case with your attorney?"

Again, Wilson answered in the affirmative.

We all sat motionless as Judge Ross continued his questioning. "Do you believe you have been fully advised by your attorney as to all aspects of your case, including your legal rights and the possible consequences of your plea to these charges?"

"Yes," he answered again.

"Do you have any questions of me?" the judge asked.

"No."

I glanced over to the other side of the courtroom and saw the lone woman looking over at us while Judge Ross continued his questioning.

"Have you understood all of the questions I asked you today, as well as the questions asked of you during your plea on November 19, 2010?"

"Yes."

The judge continued, "Do you believe your attorney has adequately, completely, and effectively represented you in your defense to these charges?"

Almost inaudibly again, Wilson said, "Yes."

"You understand that the plea agreement that was reached by your attorney and the state is going to include two consecutive life sentences, in addition to concurrent sentences, and that you will have to serve eighty-five percent on each of the life sentences before being eligible for parole?"

"Yes."

"You may now sit down and I will hear statements from the family."

I watched as the guards placed themselves on either side of Wilson, escorting him as he slowly shuffled back to his seat. All through this methodical questioning, it was nearly impossible to believe that we were living through the result of his wanton immorality.

Alvin had asked Lisa to read his statement as he had done for Kenneth Shepard's sentencing. I watched Alvin sobbing as Lisa read the following portion of his statement:

"Lorenzo Wilson is responsible for many deaths: the death of a mother, who won't be there to guide her children, attend their weddings, or be a grandmother. The death of a child who won't be able to give her loving care and devotion to her parents. The death of a sister who won't be there for the brother she adored and cherished. The death of a soul mate, who will never share her love, her life, and her dreams. The death of an invaluable friend and teacher who won't be there to inspire and share her zest for life."

David and I got up from our seats and took the long walk up to the judge's bench. We locked arms as David began his ardent statement:

"Your Honor," he said. "My name is David Schaffer, and I am the father of Susan Schaffer." His voice shook as he uttered those simple words of introduction. I held tightly onto his arm as he tried to speak while choking back his tears.

"At the outset I would like to say that my family, although not unanimously," and here I knew he was referring specifically to Rachel, "supports the prosecutor's acceptance of Wilson's guilty plea and the sentence you will be imposing on him today. Before you do that, however, I would like the opportunity to speak about my daughter, who was so brutally murdered by this defendant, and the effect her death has had on the people she left behind, family and others, who loved her and who are left to struggle with her death and the enormous grief it has caused them."

He hesitated for a moment but went on to describe Susie as a beautiful forty-eight-year-old single mother who in spite of a divorce raised three young children. He spoke about her lifelong interest in fitness, exercise, and good nutrition, describing her as someone who studied very hard and was able to build a career for herself as one of only two persons in St. Louis certified to teach the Gyrotonic system.

"In fact," David added, "just a year before her death she had taken the huge step of opening her own Gyrotonic studio and was progressing steadily to build her clientele. But the core of her life was her children. She was a consummate cook, with an exuberance and zest for life that attracted many people to her. Nothing I say can bring back my beautiful daughter. If I had my way, your honor would be giving him a death sentence, because that's what he really deserves. But on behalf of Susan and her family, I want to say that for what he has done, I hope Lorenzo Wilson's life in prison is nothing but a living hell and that he never gets out."

There was complete silence as David completed his statement. I kept glancing at the judge, whose eyes had been fixed on David while he read his statement.

I took a deep breath before it was my turn to speak. David's statement recalled Susie on a more personal level. I repeated my views on seeking justice, describing the wanton crimes against humanity, citing the sixth commandment and a portion from the book of Exodus (chapter 20:13), and discussing the sanctity of life and the fact that Susie was a symbol of these principles, while on the contrary, Lorenzo Wilson's depravity was exercised without conscience. In conclusion, I addressed the judge as follows: "Justice may be served if this perpetrator develops a conscience and endures the utmost pain and suffering as it has enveloped our family."

David put his arms around my shoulders as I completed my statement. Before we returned to our seats, I glanced at the judge and saw a sympathetic expression on his face. We sat down on either side of Eric, who leaned over and kissed the two of us. He immediately rose and walked swiftly and determinedly to place himself in front of the judge, but also directly in line with Lorenzo Wilson. Eric has the gift of eloquence. However, even I was amazed as he expressed his innermost feelings, not only for himself but for all humanity.

At Shepard's sentencing, he had spoken to the court to invoke the maximum sentence allowed by law. This time, his remarks were directed to the defendant.

Eric began:

> "Lorenzo Wilson. You truly are a completely worthless piece of ectoplasm. You don't get to be called a human being because you don't qualify as one. If you were so interested in stealing computers, iPods, and digital cameras, why didn't you just do that instead of shooting her? If you think about it, rather

than sitting here on the precipice of going to jail for the next fifty years, you would have been charged with burglary and perhaps served a few years or, even better, gotten off with probation. But no, I guess you weren't capable of doing that very simple calculation. Stupid is not even close to capturing how dumb you really are."

I glanced across the aisle and viewed that lone woman again. This time her head was bowed in her hand. There was now no doubt in my mind; she had to be Lorenzo Wilson's mother. I listened as Eric continued with his statement.

"Let's not mince words. We all know what you did was first-degree, cold-blooded murder. There's no denying that. Sure, you're going away for two consecutive life sentences because you pled to second-degree murder, but we all know what you actually did. It's because we live in an imperfect society with an imperfect legal system that you get to plead second-degree murder, but let's not be confused—you are a murderer and you committed your crime in the most vicious, cold-blooded, premeditated way. If that's not first-degree murder, I don't know what is."

Eric paused for a moment and then continued:

"I try to imagine what you did not learn and what no one taught you about the world during the previous seventeen years that would lead you to take the life of my sister. I have given this much

thought over the past twenty-four months and
have not been able to come up with an answer."

He took a deep breath, looked in Lorenzo Wilson's direction
and resumed reading his statement:

"If you wanted to take someone's life so bad, why
not take your own? Whatever it was, why didn't you
just shoot yourself? It would have satisfied your
sick, demented sense of curiosity and it would rid
the world of your worthless and pathetic presence.
What I do know is that this inhuman act you did
at age seventeen is resulting in a punishment that
will be measured in multiples of your life prior to
taking Susie's life."

Eric paused as he looked to the judge's bench and back to
Wilson, and then continued reading:

"Think very hard in jail on your (I'll do the math
for you, because I know you're not capable of doing
it yourself) thirty-fourth, fifty-first, and sixty-
eighth birthdays (if you live that long) that you
are behind bars because your evil mind chose to
ignore the difference between right and wrong in
the same society where the rest of us know right
from wrong. But you *did* know right from wrong
and were out to steal, and you looked forward to the
thrill of killing someone with your stolen handgun
if that became necessary. Shepard's confession said
it all when you handed him the gun and wanted
him to know how it feels to kill someone."

Another pause, then Eric eyed Wilson and continued again:

"Every single person in your life became completely worthless to you at the exact point that you pulled the trigger that killed my beautiful sister. There is nothing any family member of yours can say to me or any member of my family that would be worth listening to other than 'I failed and I am a complete failure.' To hear anything else is an insult to me, to my family, and most of all to my dead sister. And hasn't she been insulted enough?"

As Eric spoke, I watched him trying to keep his composure, but the trembling in his voice was a telltale sign.

"What makes this worse for me and is even more disturbing is that you had ample opportunity to change direction when you and your buddy Shepard were up to no good on December 16, 2008. After knocking on other doors in the neighborhood, you could have realized that it was wrong to burglarize someone's home. You did not. When you entered my sister's home and heard the television on, you proceeded to go into the house anyway. Most people would assume that if the television is on, the likelihood is that someone is home, and not enter in the first place. You did not. This tells me that you and your buddy were ready for action—any action—to get what you wanted. Obviously, the action you were looking for came true: you got to kill someone besides burglarizing their house. Shepard admitted that he recognized my niece from a picture on the refrigerator when he was in the kitchen pillaging for items to steal, but you told him to keep going anyway. How damaged can you be to know you are stealing from someone you know and not stop and leave? To me, all of this really reinforces a total disregard for the rules we all live by and are expected to abide by in a civilized society—a society that apparently you are not fit to be in, ever."

Eric stopped again as he raised his head from his printed statement to look first at the judge and then back at Wilson. I glanced to the other side of the room and noticed the lone woman shifting her head from hand to hand while Eric started speaking again.

"I can only imagine that the screwed-up wiring in your brain made you do what you did on December 16, 2008. I wonder if the conversation in your head goes something like this: 'Yeah, I can take this gun and go break into some empty house and take good stuff. Cool. I've been wanting some new electronics and you never know what other valuable stuff I could get. I can use it myself or sell it and get some cash. Hell, I'm entitled to it. After all, the laws of society don't apply to me. And if there's any trouble, I can always just use the gun. No one will ever catch me. I'm too smart for that.' You probably didn't ever think or have it enter into your sick little mind that it is *all completely wrong*."

My eyes met David's as our son continued his statement. I motioned for David to look at the actions of the lone woman across the aisle, which he acknowledged.

"So here you are, looking *so cool* and indifferent as you are about to be sent to a maximum security prison until you're seventy. If I'm alive, I promise you, if you make it that far (which I seriously doubt you will), I will be there to lobby at your parole hearing that society should never know you outside the walls of a maximum security prison. I know, you seem so unfazed and 'whatever.' I know you are *so tough*. We all know you are *so tough*. *Puleeze.* Truth is, we all know you are scared s--- less. Close your eyes now and think how all those rapists and murderers are going to find the new kid on the cell block. Hope you're ready for a good time, pal. You're really going to get what you have coming to you. And when (not if) you get attacked and abused, think down deep inside your f----d up little brain what got you there. That you took the life of one of the most beautiful creatures to walk the face of the earth."

Eric stopped reading as he dropped his statement to his side then said, "You are not worth taking up any space in society."

I experienced many emotions as Eric concluded his statement. David and I have always derived so much pride from both of our children, their values, and the thought processes they were always able to express. Now here was Eric, who was so articulate about the legal system and the vileness of this act. But most importantly, it was a tribute to him, his dead sister, and their loving relationship.

We all reached across to hug Eric while the judge recalled Wilson to stand at the bench once more.

Judge Ross began his questioning again. "Do you know of any reason why the court should not now pronounce sentence?"

"No," answered Wilson.

The judge continued: "No legal cause having been shown why judgment and sentence should not now be pronounced, it is then the order, sentence, and judgment of the court that the defendant, Lorenzo Wilson, be sentenced as follows: As to count one, murder in the second degree, the court sentences you to life in the custody of the Missouri Department of Corrections. As to count two, armed criminal action, the court sentences you to twenty years in the Missouri Department of Corrections concurrent to count one. As to count three, robbery first degree, the court sentences you to life in prison. This sentence will run consecutive to count one but concurrent to all other counts and continued with each of the other counts."

Again, I eyed the lone woman across the aisle. This time her head was buried between both arms.

The judge then said, "I hereby remand you to the custody of the Department of Justice Services for transportation to the Missouri Department of Corrections where you will serve out said sentence."

The judge paused for a moment and then asked Wilson, "Do you have anything to say to the court?"

"Yes," he said.

"Please," said the judge.

Wilson turned from the judge's bench to face our family. He said, "I want to apologize. I'm dumb. I'm a big failure."

We all sat speechless, remembering the police's description of him as "pure evil." I thought he might actually have felt some remorse. But it was too late for us. The guards ushered the shackled, handcuffed Wilson through the same door he had entered.

Judge Ross made his own statement from the bench. "This is the most tragic, senseless crime I have ever seen in thirty years of being involved in the system."

There was nothing more to say. However, I thought to myself, *It's no wonder Judge Ross has earned such great respect.*

Lisa gathered us together, and we all started to walk out of the courtroom. I was last in line, following Eric. I noticed the lone woman walking toward me.

"I want to talk to you," she said, pointing directly at me.

I stopped, now certain this was Lorenzo Wilson's mother. "God forgives," she said. "Please forgive him."

Eric turned around to face her.

The mother continued, "I'm a single mother. He's my only child."

Enraged, Eric yelled at her, "God has nothing to do with this, and you must have heard what I said. We will—I will—*never* forgive him!"

Upon hearing the commotion, everyone in our group rushed back into the doorway.

The mother kept repeating, "God forgives. Please forgive."

"Oh, *shut up*," Eric retorted furiously.

Lisa guided us out of the courtroom door and into the lobby. She spotted a guard and said, "Please make sure that woman stays inside the courtroom until we leave."

Safely through the door, we all gathered around Lisa. Eric encircled her in his arms and said, "You've been an extraordinary help throughout this ordeal these past two years. We could never have survived without you." I couldn't have agreed with Eric's statement more and expressed my appreciation as well.

Speaking to Lisa, I couldn't resist bringing up again the police's description of Wilson as "pure evil and cocky."

"Yes, I know, but after two years of jail he has lost his cockiness."

"May he rot," I blurted out.

Lisa nodded in agreement.

I thought about Lorenzo Wilson's mother. One journalist reported after the sentencing that she was a widow and had been fired from her job as a result of her son's crime. I felt sorry for her.

Did it make sense to fire this poor woman because of her son's crime? We will never know the answer to this question. Nor will we ever understand what could have led her son to take the life of our daughter, mother, sister, and friend.

Chapter
37

Hold fast to dreams
For if dreams die
Life is a broken-winged bird
That cannot fly.
—Langston Hughes

I believe that imagination is stronger than knowledge –
That myth is more potent than history.
I believe that dreams are more powerful than facts –
That hope always triumphs over experience –
That laughter is the cure for grief.
And I believe that love is stronger than death.
– Robert Fulghum

Dreams reflect the essence of the human soul's innermost thoughts and feelings. In some cases, they seem to involuntarily express deepened feelings after the death of a loved one. Sigmund Freud wrote, "Dreams are often most profound when they seem the most crazy." Dreams may be vivid while they are occurring, but it is astounding that they can sometimes be remembered in equally minute detail. Such was the case for David and Alvin, who exchanged the following e-mails about their respective dreams three years after Susie's death and then forwarded them to me. They considered the craziness of their experience, but both were intensely moved by what seemed so real.

David wrote:

Dear Alvin:
I don't remember if I told you about this, but I wanted to write it down. I was at Daniel's Bar Mitzvah (though this boy didn't look like Daniel). Lois and I were sitting a few rows back from the front, which had high-backed seats, so you couldn't see the backs of heads. When he was called to the bimah, there was a lot of noise from up front, as if he were looking for something he had to bring up with him. Finally, he emerged and went to the bimah with a tray of what looked like cakes and other desserts. He apologized for the delay and said it was because his mom couldn't find what he needed, or words to that effect. At this very point, Susie, who was sitting in the front row, stood. She turned around to face us all and gave that silent smile/laugh of hers as if to say, "He's right!" The look on her face was so definitely her look. The next minute she reappeared at the end of the row to the front and left of where we were sitting. This time she turned to face me directly, and her full face had a glow around it, almost a halo effect, different from everyone else. While looking at me, she mouthed the words, "Are you OK?" directly to me. I knew at that moment that she was not really there and that I wasn't OK because of that, and then I woke up.

To which Alvin replied:

David:

Thanks for telling me. I have been visited too! I don't think I've shared my dream about Susie before. I am in my house, in my bedroom. My sister is there and someone else I don't know. The TV is on and reports a story that triggered an event between Susie and me on our last Mexico vacation, and I start laughing. I hear her laughter coming from the other side of the bed, and of course I can't believe it. I'm shaking. It's Susie smiling lovingly at me. We look at each other and I jump on top of her, wrap my arms around her, and kiss her and won't let go. There's no one else in the room. It, too, was so real. I woke up in the middle of the night, realizing it was a dream, but I still feel it happened. Yes, Susie is always with us, and forever in our hearts, souls, and thoughts.

I recently closed out of my support group after three and a quarter years and told my fellow members what helped me most was staying here long enough not only to help myself, but my fellow members—and most importantly—finding a new way to love Susie that's more powerful than ever.

Perhaps Alvin and David were visited by Susie. Perhaps not. We have no real way of confirming it. However, we know their dreams were indicative of their loss, of loving, caring relationships, and how that loss has made a lasting impact on their lives, not to mention all the other lives she touched.

Chapter

38

The deaths of multitudes of people in natural disasters such as hurricanes, tornadoes, earthquakes, and tsunamis are caused by tragic acts of nature. The loss of those who perished is deeply felt by family and friends. The catastrophic deaths of the victims of 9/11 and the Holocaust feel even more devastating because they were caused by other human beings and become even more compelling when we personally relate to one individual or know someone involved. In this way, the inordinate number of people who are felled by gun violence can be compared to the Holocaust and 9/11. Focusing on one personal story brings the horror home to ordinary lives.

The Diary of Anne Frank is a perfect example. Of the millions murdered during the Holocaust, this book focuses on how the life of a single child, the promise of a bright future, was cruelly cut off. It is a glaring disparity between human morality and inhuman immorality.

Our personal story is a quintessential example of why there is an immediate need to stop the easy accessibility of illegal handguns that are ultimately appropriated by the wrong individuals.

Susie Schaffer shared many meaningful relationships: daughter, mother, life partner, teacher, and friend to many people. Like Anne Frank, Martin Luther King Jr., John Lennon, John F. Kennedy Jr., and Robert F. Kennedy, the promise of her life was brutally and suddenly ended by an unconscionable, violent act.

Our daughter was the embodiment of justice and human morality, in direct opposition to blatant violence and immorality. Susie is a symbol of the multitudes murdered by gun violence. Whatever we can do to reverse this trend will be a force to affirm and uphold the sanctity of life and hope.

My choice is to honor her life by taking political and legal action against the plague of illegal handgun possession and their easy accessibility. That is my mission.

To prevent further tragedies would be a lasting tribute to the countless victims who have been murdered—as well as a tribute to our daughter.

Photos

Susie at three

Susie at five

Susie and Eric at six and ten

Susie at fifteen

Susie at sixteen

Susie with her children Sarah, almost seven, and Daniel, eight

Rachel, Susie, Sarah, and Daniel at Rachel's Bat Mitzvah in 1998

Daniel, Rachel, Lois, and Susie together
for Rachel's Bat Mitzvah in 1998

Susie and her daughter Rachel at high school graduation

Sarah, Susie, and Daniel at the wedding of Scott, Lois
and Ben's son, to Jenny in St. Louis, September 2006

Certified Gyrotonics instructor
Susan Schaffer.

TOTAL TONING

The newest boost-your-body trend to hit STL.

By Jamie DeVillez
Photo by Steve Perotti

Celebrities like Madonna and Teri Hatcher have been doing it for years and *Forbes* named it one of the hottest fitness trends of '06. Now Gyrotonics, the latest workout trend from the East and West Coasts, has caught on in St. Louis. Often compared to Pilates, the Gyrotonic System of Movement combines yoga-like breathing elements with the fluid movements of ballet, dancing and Tai Chi and the resistance of swimming. "It's a system of energetic movement that originates from the spine and travels out to the limbs," says Anne Thomasson, owner of Body Fusion (314.409.0229), who along with Susan Schaffer (314.537.3925), serves clients through private one-on-one training sessions—they are the only two certified Gyrotonic instructors in St. Louis. Anne, who has 15 years experience in bodywork, says she personally uses the workout to tone and lengthen muscles.

Using an apparatus called the Gyrotonic Expansion System, clients use hand- and foot-operated wheelbases and suspended pulleys for resistance, which stretches, bends and moves the muscles with minimal effort. This forces the body to work as an integrated unit, emphasizing controlled resistance, which leads to increased flexibility, strength, range of motion and balance. Each session is about ninety minutes and will leave you energized and rejuvenated—it can even help alleviate chronic back and muscle pain. "After the first session, you're instantly relaxed and more aware," says Schaffer. "People who do Gyrotonics eventually stop seeing their chiropractors and their masseuses."

Article from *ALIVE STL* magazine about
the opening of Susie's Gyrotonic studio

Susie and Eric at our fiftieth wedding
anniversary celebration in June 2007

Susie and Alvin at our fiftieth wedding
anniversary celebration in June 2007

Susie and David at our fiftieth wedding
anniversary celebration in June 2007

Susie in June 2007

Susie, Rachel, and Sarah at Thanksgiving, November 2008

Afterword

Salman Rushdie said, "One of the extraordinary things about human events is that the unthinkable becomes thinkable."

It is unthinkable that one human being can willfully take the life of another. But society faces this occurrence on a daily basis. Now we are forced to think about these unnecessary deaths and what measures can be taken to prevent them.

In February 2012, as reported on CBS New York, Governor Cuomo announced a statewide objective aimed at curtailing gun violence. He outlined a multifaceted plan using $2 million to initiate varying programs such as advertising campaigns, violence intervention, toll-free tip lines, and community-based efforts encouraging citizens to report illegal firearms.

In January 2013, in the aftermath of the Sandy Hook Elementary School massacre, Governor Cuomo's compassion for the victims in Connecticut resulted in his passing the New York Secure Ammunition and Firearms Enforcement Act, commonly known as the New York SAFE Act for gun control. These measures upholding gun control were followed by similar acts in Connecticut, Colorado, and Maryland. Recognizing the importance of taking steps to reduce gun violence, the governors of these states signed new legislation. Lawmakers and society should make similar efforts aimed at steering the well-financed National Rifle Association toward sensible gun legislation.

This is a step in the right direction, but it's not enough. Sadly, this was demonstrated in April 2013, when, despite public outcry, the Senate defeated the Manchin-Toomey bill that proposed expanded background checks for gun sales.

But society can prevail. The strength demonstrated by the National Rifle Association can be matched by society's strength. I wish to impress upon readers that my objection does not include legally purchased handguns and hunting rifles by people who have permits to own them. What I find so troublesome is the National Rifle Association's unwillingness to acknowledge that their extreme, incorrect, fanatic interpretation of the Second Amendment cannot exist in the twenty-first century with the advanced weaponry made so available for those who intend to misuse it.

Our society can begin to reverse the trend of gun violence. There are organizations that are passionate about preventing the easy accessibility of handguns and in the process save lives. They face the unthinkable on a daily basis and devote untold time and effort to preserving humanity. We can join them. We can pool our strength in a positive manner to reverse the unthinkable.

The organizations are listed below:

NEW YORKERS AGAINST GUN VIOLENCE
(NYAGV)
87 Lafayette Street
Third Floor
New York, New York 10013

GUN FREE KIDS
P.O. Box 726
Croton Falls, New York 10519

THE BRADY CAMPAIGN TO PREVENT
GUN VIOLENCE
1225 I Street NW
Suite 1100
Washington, DC 20005

MAYORS AGAINST ILLEGAL GUNS
www.mayorsagainstillegalguns.org

Unlawful deaths caused by gun violence can be addressed by educating ourselves and passing laws that make it harder for criminals, convicted felons, and the mentally ill to obtain guns. Society can lobby for stricter background checks on all gun sales and steps to strengthen law enforcement's efforts to stop illegal gun sales. As individuals, we can talk to our families, friends, and neighbors about reversing this escalating, horrific trend. Additionally, we can become involved in those organizations listed above. Contributions to any of these organizations would be gratefully appreciated. Just a little passion from everyone can help preserve a life. Eric's reaction was succinct after the defeat of the Manchin-Toomey bill in the U.S. Senate for gun-ownership background checks. His comment was, "If we don't take action, there will be many more Susies."

About the Author

Activist, dance enthusiast, coordinator, administrator, and grants writer for nonprofit organizations, Lois Schaffer has devoted her energies to protecting human rights. Her activism prompted her to participate in marches and rallies in support of the civil rights movement and to protest the war in Vietnam. She was actively advocating the reduction of gun violence even before her daughter's murder. Now her energies are even more focused to honor her daughter's memory and prevent tragedies for other families.

Lois's nonprofit, grant writing, and administrative duties included writing proposals for the Pearl Lang Dance Foundation Inc. and supporting low-income housing for seniors. Her ongoing mission to reduce gun violence has included speaking about sensible gun legislation to various local and national groups and attending press conferences, gun-control rallies, and the legislative hearings on gun control in Connecticut after the Newtown massacre. This book is indicative of her commitment and concern for others.

Lois and her husband David live in Great Neck, Long Island. They have a son and six grandchildren.